The Embodied Word

The Embodied Word
Preaching as Art and Liturgy

CHARLES L. RICE

FORTRESS PRESS   MINNEAPOLIS

THE EMBODIED WORD
Preaching as Art and Liturgy

Library of Congress Cataloging-in-publication Data
Rice, Charles Lynvel, 1936–
    The embodied word : preaching as art and liturgy / Charles L. Rice.
      p. cm. — (Fortress resources for preaching)
    Includes bibliographical references.
    ISBN 0-8006-2453-X (alk. paper)
    1. Preaching. 2. Liturgics. I. Title. II. Series.
BV4211.2.R47   1991
251—dc20   90-21915
                                                        CIP

The paper used in this publication meets the minimum requirements of American National Standard for Information Sciences—Permanence of Paper for Printed Library Materials, ANSI Z329.48-1984   (∞)™

Manufactured in the U.S.A.   AF 1-2453

95   94   93   92   91   1   2   3   4   5   6   7   8   9   10

To Robert B. Barker

Far from being merely an instruction or a religious talk, the homily is an act inherent to the rhythmic ritual of the liturgy.

—Aidan Kavanagh, *Elements of Rite*

The sermon is a part of the liturgy itself.

—Vatican II, *Constitution on the Sacred Liturgy*

Contents

Preface

This book describes the situation of preaching, how things stand with the pulpit in North America in this last decade of the twentieth century, and proposes a more intentionally liturgical, specifically sacramental orientation for the sermon. This proposal is directed not only to those whose churches would describe themselves as liturgical but also to anyone who feels the preacher's need for language that springs from a community's life, for a sense of connection between the community and the sermon, and for more modest but clearer goals for preaching. How can we strengthen the connection between preaching and the community? Could the answer to that question be, at least in part, liturgical? Does freedom for imaginative and prophetic communication lie in more closely connecting preaching to the sacraments?

In this inquiry, I ask the indulgence of those for whom the practice of my own denomination might be unfamiliar. I hope to keep the ear of those whose churches do not have Holy Communion weekly. Although it is true that most of my own preaching is at the Eucharist, I know by experience the presence of the Word of God in the simplest service of Scripture and preaching, singing and prayer, which has been normative for a majority of American churches. This book comes out of my own growing understanding of worship that makes more of Holy Communion, at least in frequency and ceremony, than my own forebears practiced. I do not, however, assume that I understand the Eucharist better or practice it more profoundly than did my Baptist grandmother, who drank a tiny glass of grape juice every three months and for whom sermons, two every Sunday, were, in some unaccountable way, sacramental. In fact, I have hardly experienced better liturgy than in that small-town Oklahoma church, where everyone knew what to do and how to do it with warmth and dignity, right down to singing the hymns "by heart."

The last thing I wish to do is to take one more step in the direction of distancing those who care about preaching from those who are intentional about liturgy. What I do want is to bring my own experience, both as a preacher and as one on a spiritual journey, to the service of those who, in their own unique places, seek to speak of God where people gather to worship. In all of those places, city and country, there are most likely a table and a font not too far from the pulpit. Everyone who preaches is not that far from Baptism and Eucharist, whatever the frequency of their celebration in a given congregation. That proximity and a renewed sense of the sacramental ethos of Christian faith have many implications, especially for preachers.

Chapter 1 describes the relationship between Word and Sacrament and the integration of those in the offices of pastor, prophet, and priest. Chapter 2 considers the consequences in the American pulpit of the split between Word and Sacrament, and chapter 3 argues that a primary function of the sermon is liturgical, standing as it does between Scripture on the one hand and Sacrament on the other. Chapter 4 shows how image and story, particularly as seen in the parables of Jesus, serve a sacramental understanding of the Word. Chapter 5 makes the case that the liturgical setting for preaching both enables and limits the use of the arts in the pulpit, especially literature, drama, and cinema. Chapter 6 provides concrete examples and makes specific suggestions for preparing and delivering sermons that are worthy companions to the liturgy.

I was born into a family deeply steeped in Baptist traditions, and I was first ordained "a preacher" (as my people would say) in that denomination. I served for twenty years as a minister of the United Church of Christ, whose watchword I honor, "that they may all be one." Now I am a priest of the Episcopal Church, serving as pastoral associate in a parish in New Jersey, where I also teach in a seminary of the United Methodist Church. This book comes from that journey and is indebted to more people, in all of those churches, than I could name.

I am indebted especially to Dean Thomas Ogletree of the Theological School of Drew University, for his support, and to Professor Paul Scott Wilson, Emmanuel School of Theology, Toronto, for the care and candor of a colleague and friend. I am grateful to the late Dr. John Hollar, of Fortress Press, for his encouragement over many years and especially in preparing this book.

Madison, New Jersey
All Saints' Day, 1990

1
Pulpit and Table

The Lord be with you.
And also with you.
Lift up your hearts.
We lift them to the Lord.
Let us give thanks to the Lord our God.
It is right to give God thanks and praise.
It is right, and a good and joyful thing, always and everywhere to
    give thanks.
                                     —*The Book of Common Prayer*

About forty men and women had gathered for the early service, around a free-standing altar in a side chapel of St. Luke's
Episcopal Church. Members of the congregation read lessons from
the Hebrew Scriptures and Paul's writings. The priest in charge
read the Gospel and then invited me, the visiting preacher, to
the table to give the sermon. Although I had lectured many times
on Karl Barth's definition of proclamation as "preaching and the
sacraments," and on Justin Martyr's account of the second-century
"president" of the Eucharist preaching at the table, I found myself unprepared for the experience.[1] For a moment I stood silently,
trying, as it were, to put my homiletical feet under the table. The
typewritten pages lay awkwardly on the altar cloth, and the sermon
I had prepared seemed out of scale, rather like giving a speech to
one's family, holding forth at the dinner table. I had written the
sermon to be delivered from the pulpit, but now I stood at the table
in the midst of the people. What was momentarily unsettling led
to a homily different in both content and delivery from the one I
had prepared, and to further reflection on the interrelatedness of

preaching and the sacramental community gathered around baptistry and table. This book is, in part, an expanded engagement of the questions that surfaced that Sunday morning.

A PLACE TO STAND

Many have experienced the split between preaching and liturgy, especially the distance between pulpit and altar. In North America the pulpit predominates the table; for a majority of North American Christians, the service of the table continues to be, despite liturgical renewal, an element of, or even an addendum to, the service of the pulpit. But as the liturgies of most of the churches give a larger and more frequent place to the Eucharist, preachers are looking for a place to stand that is spiritually and spatially closer to the table, more a part of the liturgy.

For some, the very word *liturgy* may signal caution: Cannot undue emphasis upon liturgical form and practice lead us away from devoted preaching? Focusing on ritual to the neglect of the sermon is a danger no less common than spending the time and energy on administrative matters that a pastor ought to direct to homiletical preparation. Properly understood and executed liturgy, however, can provide the focus, continuity, and support that many preachers are seeking. The definition of liturgy, "the work of the people," points us in the direction of making vital connections with an active community that can stimulate, direct, and sustain the preacher. The truly liturgical environment is always at work; liturgy is never passive. It is as deeply involved in giving thanks to God in Christ as in acting out that gratitude in service to the world. The preacher's place is at that intersection of liturgy and the world, where one can be both prophet and pastor, always in the context of being a priest.

"Churches," Aidan Kavanagh says categorically, "are not carpeted." Liturgy, he says, needs "hardness, sonority, and a certain bracing discomfort much like the Gospel itself."[2] Liturgical voices—praying, singing, declaiming—require an environment of acoustical vigor, that feeling of vibrant resonance one gets singing a hymn of Charles Wesley in a Methodist church built of wood, stone, and glass. The preacher's voice, too, demands this liturgical resonance.

I recall the first time I preached from an ideally constructed pulpit, in St. Michael's Church in Manhattan. This pulpit is perched atop a flight of curving stairs and is at a considerable height above the congregation. At first consideration, this might suggest distance, even aloofness. But, in fact, this pulpit is built entirely of stone and is tied in to the whole building architecturally, by its structure and placement well into the nave. The feeling, standing on a resonant surface under a large, wooden sounding board, is one of connection. I was preaching from the soles of my feet, which seemed connected to the whole building and to everyone sitting there. The opposite of this would be standing on a plush carpet at a disconnected podium or, at farthest remove, speaking to a television camera.

Preaching in St. Michael's pulpit (the preacher is led to it and is given a drink of water just before climbing the stairs!) is both like and unlike standing at the corner of the holy table giving a homily early on a Sunday morning. In that high pulpit the preacher could lose her or his feet and become caught up in self-conscious oratory, losing sight of both table and congregation; high pulpits may invite homiletical strutting and rhetorical distancing. It may be such possibilities that have led some preachers to abandon the pulpit for close-up discourse, while others welcome such an exalted position for giving lengthy, oratorical sermons.

For my own part, standing in that venerable pulpit, feeling physically connected to the building and the people, was like standing at the altar when (to use the language of contemporary psychology) the liturgy is "in flow," when one cannot tell work from play, when ability and task are on a similar plane, when time becomes irrelevant. It is this experience that describes both preaching and liturgy at their best. When this occurs (in the case of preaching when the homily becomes "an act inherent to the rhythmic ritual of the liturgy"), we see how closely related are the embodiment of the Word by the preacher in the pulpit and the embodiment of the Word by the priest at the altar, whose voice and body speak for the whole community.

If the experience at the table at St. Luke's Church helped me to understand the need to bring the pulpit and altar closer together, then my experience in the pulpit at St. Michael's helped me realize how that might be done: The key is focusing on the embodied

Word. The latter experience reinforced my sense that in preaching and sacrament the Word is embodied, in preacher as in priest. One of the aims of this book, then, is to point to ways of fostering the link between the embodiment of the Word in the preacher and in the priest, and I am particularly interested in exploring how we might make sermons more "liturgy-friendly." The undergirding thesis of this book is that the sermon can stand on its own apart from the sacraments no more than Baptism and Eucharist can continue with integrity apart from Scripture and preaching. Hence the central questions we must take up are these: Can we find a place and a way to preach that faithfully resonate the Word of God seeking embodiment in bread, wine, water, human speech, and a community's interaction? Can we find a way of preaching that helps make all these factors and experiences an inseparable whole?

These questions are put primarily to the preacher. That seems fitting, in that for most clergy in North America it is the sermon that has fared better in the schism of Word and Sacrament, at least in terms of attention and the allocation of time in the Sunday service. Also, preachers are becoming increasingly aware of the growing isolation of the sermon and of the unrealistic demands made of them. Preaching needs, by all indications, more liturgical support from those who come to hear it, and it needs for its context the enacted embodiment of the sacraments. So, we will move from the perspective of the preacher to ask what it means that the sacraments are the context and companion of preaching. The case will be made that the sermon is part of the liturgy, that it is most appropriately given, as it were, at the table, with the baptistry always in view, and that it moves toward and is finally completed in Holy Communion.

THE END OF THE SERMON

The word *end* is used here with deliberate ambiguity—the end as both limit and aim—to suggest that the form, style, and content of preaching might be reshaped by bringing the preacher closer to the table. We may say that the Eucharist is the end of the sermon in at least three senses. First, the aim of the homily is to bring people to make Eucharist, to speak of our life together in the light of Scripture in a way that leads the congregation toward thanksgiving and enables that to happen. The sermon is one movement in the liturgical action of the community, and in every case the aim of that movement is great thanksgiving. Second, the sermon is defined, its limits are set, by the Eucharist, by the essential gospel that is embodied there. The person who preaches with the table in view may not preach on just anything or without regard for style appropriate to this setting. The sacramental context, both Baptism and Holy Communion, judges preaching, sets limits to it, calls to account mere sermonizing and pulpiteering, the inordinate preaching of the law and indiscriminate use of the pulpit for promotion or for calling attention to cultural observances. Where our preaching presupposes Baptism and proclaims what the Eucharist sets forth, we are less likely to forget who we are and why we are preaching. Third, the homily is completed in the Eucharist. As almost every preacher would agree, no sermon worth preaching seems complete in itself. Does not the sermon find its conclusion as members of the community gather around the table in the anamnesis of Jesus, to lift up their hearts in praise and thanks to God?

From Baptism to Eucharist

The origin of preaching is Baptism, and the aim of the sermon is Eucharist. The preacher stands between font and table, Scripture in hand, leading the people once more, because of and in spite of all that may have happened that week, to renew their Baptism and come to the table. This is not unlike the family dinner table, to which we may come because we belong to the family and to which we need to come, even when things are not going well, to eat and drink, remember who we are, and find the courage and strength of shared gratitude. The obligation of the preacher to enable this movement—from Scripture to home and marketplace, to hospital, school, and graveyard, and finally to lifting up the heart to God— gives to preaching a twofold position, always holding together the reality of life in the flesh and the call to faithful prayer. This crucial act calls for embodiment, a person who lives with the community, who experiences and articulates the people's suffering, and who leads them to give thanks nevertheless. Karl Barth, preaching on Ps. 73:23 ("Nevertheless I am continually with thee"), built a sermon around this idea. He concluded with this prayer: "We spread out everything before thee . . . our whole life in this our time, that thou wouldst lead it to the resurrection of the body and the life everlasting."[3] Have we seen the connection, and the essential similarity, between the sermon, that unique vehicle for spreading out our life, and the call to come to the table laid before us?

The sermon has an indispensable liturgical function, to enable the congregation to face their actual situation in the world and at all times and in all places give thanks to God in Christ. Although the sermon might from time to time have a didactic, hortatory, evangelistic, or even promotional agenda, its primary goal is set by its place in the community's worship, between the reading of Scripture and the call to bring an offering and come to the table. This position suggests the form of preaching as inductive[4] and its content as both biblical and secular.

Even in churches where the Eucharist is not celebrated every Sunday, this orientation of pulpit to table is being recognized. For example, the sermon is less likely at present to occur at the end of the service, as if everything built up to that. Placing the sermon between the reading of Scripture and the offertory, before the prayers, is one way of recognizing the function of preaching: to enable people to face the world and then to give themselves once more to God. Even when the community does not break bread, the liturgical function of preaching is not entirely lost. The preacher serves the most important work of the people, to gather up all that is and to come in grateful prayer before God.

Sacrament as Homiletical Canon

The second sense in which the Eucharist is the end of the preaching is that every sermon is judged by it. In the long history of preaching it has often been said, and virtually everywhere assumed, that preaching is judged by Scripture, a contention that we must surely honor. Whatever one's view of the inspiration of Scripture, it is certainly the most reliable record of the primary witnesses to Jesus as the Christ. On that basis we will continue to require that preaching be faithful to the essential and comprehensive testimony of Scripture. The preacher listens to the Bible for the voice of those earliest witnesses, the voice of the church, and even the voice of Jesus; and it is out of this attentiveness that authentic proclamation rises.

But even more than the canon of Scripture, it is the sacraments—in particular Holy Communion—that hold the preacher to Jesus Christ, by whom all Scripture, tradition, and preaching are judged. Beyond even the requirement for faithful exegesis, theological reflection, and hermeneutical integrity, it is the liturgical setting and aim of preaching that finally weigh its merits. The presence of Christ at the holy table does not admit just any kind of preaching. Rather, if we follow Luther (and Barth after him), just as Jesus Christ is host at the Eucharist, only Christ is, finally, the true preacher. Luther puts it this way: "Now I and any who speaketh Christ's Word may freely boast that his mouth is Christ's mouth. I am certain that my word is not mine but Christ's word, therefore my mouth must all be His whose word it speaketh."[5]

All of us who preach need to be heartened by this when our preaching seems ineffective, but it should also chasten us when we find ourselves the center of attention and unduly concerned for the bows to our egos that can come from preaching. The sacramental setting of preaching keeps the preacher reminded of what is at the same time the limitation of preaching—that it is the continuation of the preaching of Christ—and its liberation; that setting liberates preaching because it frees the preacher from all preoccupations that are unworthy of the broken and triumphant one present to us in bread and wine. For Barth, as for the Reformers, when we say "Word of God" we mean Jesus Christ present to his people, and without that neither Scripture nor preaching opens toward God's eventful Word. Barth quotes Luther on the prior knowledge of Christ that is necessary to Scripture's efficacy as Word of God: "To have scripture without knowledge of Christ is to have no Scripture, and is none other than to let this star shine and not perceive it."[6] The place to read Scripture, like the place to preach, is close to the table, where the church knows most assuredly the presence of Christ the host. We must, as we preach and listen to preaching, as Luther said, "look at the contents of God's hand stretched out to us in Him."[7]

Thus, the sacraments, Baptism no less than Holy Communion, stand in judgment of any usurpation of the office of preaching by a cult of personality. The conflict between liturgy and preaching is, at base, the unresolved tension in Western Protestantism between sacramental community and heroic individualism. This should not lead us away from what is so obvious about preaching, that the Word of God comes through real human beings. Phillips Brooks's definition remains true: "Preaching is the communication of truth through personality."[8] But in thousands of churches people go to church to hear the Reverend So-and-So, and on the infrequent communion Sunday, they stay away. These churches center, more or less, on a personality, and preaching is in many cases the means of perpetuating this situation. The results are idiosyncratic sermons, emphasis on issues and causes that may have only marginal connection with the gospel, undue promotionalism, a parochial moral and ethical perspective, and the self-serving single-issue diatribe.

What is amiss here is that preaching has lost its proper ground; it has been removed from the place where we receive God's Word from the outstretched hand of Christ, whose Word is served equally by preacher and priest. Baptism reminds the preacher that this congregation is marked as Christ's own forever, that their life in Christ is prior to the sermon of the day. The presence of the Eucharist calls the preacher back to the essential gospel—to the saving grace of God in the crucified and risen Lord—and away from what Luther called "the word of man":

> As often as the Word of God is preached, it makes men's consciences before God happy, broad, and certain, because it is a word of grace and forgiveness, a good and beneficial word. As often as the word of man is preached, it makes men's consciences in themselves sad, narrow, and anxious, because it is a word of law, wrath, and sin, pointing to what man has not done and all that he ought to do.[9]

At the table, where Christ is the preacher and where all we receive is from his outstretched and inviting hands, the preaching of the law, "the word of man," is excluded. The preacher, in this position, whatever issues and ideas may clamor for attention, cannot ignore the palpable presence of the table, to which, after the preacher has stopped speaking, all will be freely invited. This, like the presence of the baptistry, judges every sermon by the untrammeled grace of the gospel. In the middle of how many sermons would both congregation and preacher be rescued from something less than the gospel by casting an eye toward the baptistry, or by hearing the words "Christ invites to his table all . . ."?

The Finishing Touch

The third sense in which the Eucharist is the end of the sermon is that preaching is finally completed at the table. The church in which I grew up—which, though I did not know even the word at the time, had its own well-developed liturgy—assumed that every sermon would end in the invitation. The preacher would fade the sermon into this climactic moment and then come down from the pulpit to await those coming forward (usually to the singing of a gospel hymn such as "Just as I Am") to give their hands to the minister and their lives to Christ. It would have been highly unusual in that denomination for the service to end otherwise, and the sermon that did not move toward this moment would have been considered incomplete.

In historical perspective, this parallels closely the completion of the sermon at the Eucharist. Protestant Christianity has generally substituted the evangelical invitation or the "altar call" for the weekly celebration of the Eucharist, but even in this substitution Protestantism has retained the sense that the sermon's conclusion lies beyond the preacher's speech. When all is said and done, it is the presence of the inviting, forgiving, empowering Christ, the one who speaks peace even as he sends us out into the world in his name, which is the true end of the sermon.

Most preachers upon reflection would probably agree: We seldom have the sense that a sermon is finished, that it can stand alone. One explanation for the persistent interest in the sermon as "dialogue" is that it stems from this dissatisfaction with the sermon as a free-standing piece. There is simply the need for the sermon to go somewhere in the community, to issue in an event that involves the people in their own apprehension and articulation of the gospel. In more traditional liturgies the first act following the sermon is the creed, a time for all to stand up and declare their faith. Also, the prayers, when they follow the sermon, provide a similar opportunity for the people to do their own work in the light of the sermon, to carry forward the liturgy—including the sermon—to its conclusion, a corporate experience of the presence of Christ. Some pastors assess how fruitful their sermons are by the participation of the people in the prayers, in their responses to the biddings.

But it is at the Eucharist that what we preach—if we keep our feet and stick to the proclamation of the gospel—is most unavoidably seen and heard. Here we cannot sidestep the quintessential gospel, as we reiterate God's loving purpose in creation, the broad sweep of the history of salvation in the account of Israel, and the salvation offered in the life, death, and resurrection of Jesus Christ, who is now present with us in the most comprehensive yet simplest way, in broken bread and wine poured out. Whatever the preacher has said, however limited the text or provincial the sermon, despite our homiletical failings and corporate waywardness, here we are all invited to bring the burdens and triumphs of our lives as we hear the story and give thanks in the breaking of the bread.

This realization, that the sermon is completed in the eucharistic drama, can be very liberating. The preacher cannot preach the whole Gospel story. It is not possible for the sermon to carry the weight of the entire tradition. There is in the redeeming story, from God's loving creation to the redemption in Christ, more than can possibly be put in so many words. The sermon takes its place in the liturgy, as one absolutely crucial moment in the holy work of God's people, but as a piece that cannot stand alone. That lays on the preacher a sacred duty while at the same time relieving the sermon and preacher of undue burden. The burden is no longer so heavy when the preacher realizes that the community, finally, will tell itself the story in its eucharistic feast and that Christ, by the power of the Holy Spirit, must do the preaching.

FROM CONSENSUS TO COMMUNITY

This reintegration of Word and Sacrament becomes particularly important for the church today. In an increasingly pluralistic society, communities are less likely to cohere around the pulpit or to come to healthy consensus on pressing, complex issues. We find ourselves far from the situation of the early Puritans. Harry Stout recently described them as a homogeneous culture for whom the sermon could function as "social sacrament."[10] More than ever we are dependent upon the artful liturgy to embody the gospel and to bring to clarity the essential message that we preach. The less social consensus we have, the less the pulpit will be able to get a hearing around culturally relative issues or to substitute for the saving gospel merely partial loyalties. The preacher will have to rely, more and more, like the Christian community itself, upon liturgy— the enactment in a community of what it most deeply believes—for the apprehension of the gospel and the completion of the sermon.

Placement and Presence

Placement and presence are the terms Joseph Sittler used to describe the sacramental community: "Baptism is a placement, and the Holy Communion is a presence—and that placement is a miracle of grace for [we] who have no claims upon it; and that presence is a miracle of grace for [we] who cannot create but only acknowledge creation and have creative joy in it."[11] This is precisely where the preacher stands, in a community defined by the sacraments of placement and presence. Sittler actually raises the question whether preaching, as "a lively art of the church," can be taught at all.[12] The fundamental things, he asserts, are the placement of the preacher in a community—the preacher begins as a baptized person—and the formation of the preacher as a communicant. Authentic preaching is simply the creative and faithful act of a person living out the faith in a community. In other words, no authentic preaching occurs apart from the eucharistic community, which is itself constantly being formed by the presence of God in Christ as known in Word and Sacrament. "The word is our Lord Jesus Christ himself as the concretion in redemptive action of the love of the Creator for his creature—and if the preaching of the word is not thus centered, it cannot avoid being swallowed up by categories of moral counsel or religious idealism."[13]

The preacher stands in the same place where every Christian is placed and formed, as baptized and called to Eucharist. This is the concrete reality of Christian experience, and it is this same reality that forms the preacher and that tests each sermon.

Priest in Community

In order for homiletical and liturgical language to be effective, it must be concrete. In sermons we look for concreteness; liturgy depends upon sacramental materiality and particularity; and our very faith centers on the confession of the Word become flesh. The idea of priesthood, too, depends upon this sense of corporeal and particular embodiment of the gospel. Phillips Brooks's definition of preaching—the truth of God being mediated through a person—relates as much to the priesthood as it does to Christianity itself. Although we might be inclined to shy away from this, to preach the embodied Word we need to recover the idea of the priest in community.[14] It is this person, formed in and organically connected to the sacramental community, who is the preacher. This, again, is the language of Joseph Sittler, who frequently uses the metaphor of organic connection to describe preaching: Preaching is "organic to the entire actuality of the preacher" living in a community at a particular time and place. Sittler defines preaching as "a function of the preacher's whole existence, concentrated at the point of declaration and interpretation."[15] This type of language locates priesthood in the community; it identifies the priest with a people and the internalization of their language and rituals; this image of the priest is the one we come upon in Margaret Craven's novel *I Heard the Owl Call My Name* and in Graham Greene's *The Power and the Glory*.[16] This language and these images could be appropriated more widely, regardless of denomination, much to the benefit of those who preach. This point was illuminated for me by an experience of priesthood that I had in Greece; what I witnessed reveals something of what it is to be a pastor, something particularly important for the preacher.

The experience occurred on a trip by boat from Piraeus to Santorini, a voyage that takes about twelve hours and makes as many stops, at one small island after another, to deliver the mail and take on passengers and cargo. From the upper deck the traveler gets a bird's-eye view of village life in these small ports. At every stop the local priest came down to meet the boat. Fascinated by this, I stationed myself to watch the little coveys of villagers, stevedores, and would-be passengers who clustered around the unmistakable figure in flowing black. What I began to see was that every person in the group would, at some point during the lively talk and laughter surrounding the priest, reach out to touch him. It was a small gesture, quite casual really, but an essential part of this ritual. It might be no more than to lay a hand on the priest's arm or to brush his shoulder, but it was there as predictably as a piece of the Sunday liturgy. I was looking at the embodied faith, the presence of Christ being acted out in simple human intercourse, amid the morning's commerce and the smell of the day's catch.

Those dockside dramas suggest the implications for preaching of the church as the body of Christ, particularly in its sacramental manifestations. Preaching—almost every book on homiletics from H. H. Farmer's *The Servant of the Word*[17] to the present would agree—has a stake in personal transaction. Have we considered carefully what it means to preach as an organic part of the body of Christ, as a person who is bonded in a special connection to a specific group of people? What happens when the sermon loses this priestly and pastoral connection, and what are the particular signs of that in the American experience?

2
The American Situation

When Emerson decided, in 1832, that he could no longer celebrate the Lord's Supper unless the bread and wine were removed,
an important step in the vaporization of religion in America was
taken, and the spirit of that step has continued apace.
—Flannery O'Connor, *Mystery and Manners*

The ad appeared in the *Santa Ana Register* and we went, back in
the 1950s in southern California, to hear the first sermon Robert
Schuller gave out of doors. The young preacher, Bible in hand, stood
on the roof of the Orange Drive-in Theater. It was a truly American experience, as the subsequent success of the Garden Grove
Community Church would show. There we were, in response to
an ad in the paper, sitting in our own cars listening to an attractive
and persuasive young man with a Bible. This event was as indifferent to the audience's affiliation with a church as it was attentive
to practical matters: We could see that a good many of our neighbors were on their way to or from the beach. Although everyone
present regarded this "drive-in" church as novel, hardly anyone
would have questioned its appropriateness, certainly not the theology of preaching that lay behind such an occasion. It is still the
case, as it has been for a long time in this country, that the only
prerequisites for preaching are a Bible and an audience, be it on
a corner of Times Square, at some unsuspecting proselyte's front
door, or, most importantly, on radio or television.

WITHOUT LITURGICAL FETTERS

In his short history of preaching, Yngve Brilioth describes the
great variety of the American pulpit, but he sees a notable con-

sistency: "Freedom from all liturgical fetters is perhaps the most evident and the most common basic characteristic of American preaching in every era."[1] More important than questions of liturgy, which are at bottom questions of ecclesiology, is the concern, according to Brilioth, for what is practically edifying and emotionally compelling. This "pushes the great fact of salvation in the history of revelation into the background."[2] If it is true, as is generally accepted, that Americans are first and foremost individualists, and that what we find most interesting is the friendly person who gets things done—even if it is the huckster—then it is predictable that our homiletical history would emerge in the forms in which we see it today, especially in the personalities who exploit the electronic media.[3] How would preaching resist taking its shape from the national emphasis on individual personality (often construed in the language of "freedom") and supreme confidence in what works, including those many and various hucksters who can sell the goods?

The Unfettered Personality

One of our greatest preachers, Phillips Brooks, more than a century ago defined preaching as "the communication of truth through personality."[4] Were Brooks lecturing today on preaching, he would probably substitute the word *personhood*, for the very reason that "personality" is so congenial to the American experience. In fact, it is the personality that interests us most, fully as much in the pulpit as in politics. What this means is that the notion of preaching as organic to a corporate body is foreign to our experience of preachers and preaching. The resistance to what Brilioth calls "liturgical fetters" is first of all a matter of cultural bias, or national temperament. In revivalism, a distinctly American and staunchly antiliturgical phenomenon, we see most clearly the amalgam of individualism and a self-promoting hucksterism that focuses on the personality of the preacher and the salvation of the individual soul. In a more modern form, such self-promotion emerges in what is being called "the electronic church," although, admittedly, in that phenomenon the notion of individual "salvation" has been turned largely toward "self-realization."

Much of North American Protestantism is still strongly influenced by revivalism—its moralism, promotionalism, individualism, and its antiliturgical bias. Even the Sunday worship in many churches derives its order from the methods of Charles Finney and other nineteenth-century revivalists. For example, the sermon occurs at the end of the service, with all of the other elements leading up to it, often in such a way as to focus worship on the preacher and the sermon, a kind of homiletical ocean liner preceded by a few liturgical tugboats. The service then culminates in the call to come forward (an obvious substitution for the invitation to meet Christ, in the company of sisters and brothers, at the eucharistic table). Whole congregations are organized around this moment of "joining the church," often obscuring the aim of worship and neglecting the nurturing and feeding of the community. This is the legacy of a relatively modern, distinctly American phenomenon, although many churchgoers would identify revivalism's vestiges with "the old-time religion."

A Question of Ecclesiology

I have said that liturgy is at bottom a question of ecclesiology: We worship according to the way we understand the nature of the church. That is, of course, a matter of reciprocity: With communities as with architecture we form our churches, erect our buildings, and then they form us. But even where forms of worship are ill-considered and poorly done, even at their most clerical and pretentious, they remain in some important sense—to use the most common definition of "liturgy"—the work of the people. The Sunday worship in which the preacher dominates, preaching a long sermon and managing most of the rest of the service, reflects the ecclesiology of that congregation, just as a quarterly "observance" of Holy Communion reveals a community's self-understanding.

The difficulty in altering liturgical practice stems from this fact that the attitudes and patterns of the congregation and preacher are mutually reinforcing: The leader is sensitized to the congregation's self-understanding and responds in such a way as to reinforce that. Many of the transactions at the church door are "quality checks," determining whether or not this mutual reinforcement has occurred once more. "Good sermon, Pastor," can carry many messages. This brings us again to one of the difficult questions facing us throughout this book: How does the sermon function in the community? And the answer lies in part in the point just sketched: The sermon's function, like that of every part of worship, is finally a question of ecclesiology.

The last three houses of worship to open in our area are not called churches, but chapels. Across the country they are going up, looking like church buildings, but the sign out front avoids the word *church*. The sign might say something like "Chapel in the Hills" or, very frequently, simply "Bible Chapel" or "Bible Fellowship." One could compare this with the distinction between established "church" and nonconformist "chapel" that marked the English Reformation or, more recently, with the populist notion of "antigovernment politics." The least optimistic analysis would be that these groups reject in name and practice the "one, holy, catholic, and apostolic church," preferring the more distinctly American emphasis on independence, the Bible, and a fellowship of like-minded people. It would be a mistake to generalize unduly, but at the very least we can see the vitality of the American way: continued splintering of Christian adherents into homogeneous groups that are at the same time anti-ecclesiastical and sometimes more affirming of American cultural values than of the traditions and practices of the church catholic.

Scripture and Sacrament

An open Bible is often seen on the communion table in many churches, another example of the direct line from ecclesiology to liturgical practice. One would have to surmise in seeing such a powerful symbol that the primary relationship of the people who worship there is to a book. To put this in liturgical perspective, consider an example from architectural history. Many of our churches are modeled on the Roman basilica, the great audience rooms constructed at the empire's seats of power and designed to announce authority. These vast rectangular halls, as high as they were wide, were characterized by the semicircular apse at the end opposite the entrance. Anyone entering this great room would understand immediately that the emperor's representative, sitting in the apse and dominating all this space, embodied awesome power. When the Christians (after Constantine) took over the audience halls, they simply placed the bishop's chair and the holy table in this apse.

There could be no question who was now Lord: It was Jesus Christ, present at the table and in the person of his vicar. What does it mean, in one of our churches today, when a book assumes this place? Or a pulpit?

A relationship to the Bible may be as close as millions of Christians in North America come to some tangible experience of the presence of Christ. Is this too much to say? The Bible is, after all, something that I can hold in my hands, see with my eyes, even personalize by adding to its pages my pious jottings and the history of my family. I can possess the Bible by learning its intimate secrets and by memorizing its verses and chapters. Is it any surprise that in the absence of material symbols of the faith and with the secularization of clergy and the infrequent celebration of the Eucharist, the Bible would appear at the focal point of worship? The book becomes not so much a "paper pope," as some would say, as a palpable, material bearer of the tenets of faith, in effect a sacrament. In that way of seeing it, the holy table is the obvious place for its display!

Thomas Ogletree, concerned for the use of the Bible in making ethical decisions, argues against misconstruing the authority of Scripture and its place in the religious life. His work is of singular importance for preaching, especially his effort to take Scripture seriously while placing it in proper context. What we aim at is to remove the Bible from the communion table and dispel the idea that the texts are what ultimately concern us. As someone has said, we are called not to preach the text but the gospel, and by doing so we give the Scriptures their proper place in the community. As Ogletree puts it, "We begin our discourse with texts from within our own life situations," and the aim is an enlargement of understanding concerning that about which the texts speak.[5] Put in terms of embodiment, we need to move away from the rationalism and abstract moralism into which biblicism often falls, toward Scripture read in and for a vitally engaged sacramental community. The table of Christ and the chair of his flesh-and-blood vicar are at the center. The community they embody is then served by Scripture.

Harry Emerson Fosdick, founding minister of the Riverside Church and teacher of preaching, used similar language about both Scripture and preaching. He described his own homiletics as "life-situation preaching," and he chided the church for undue preoccupation with Scripture as such. We are out of touch, he once said, if we think that people come to church on Sunday morning with a burning desire to know what happened to the Jebusites. Fosdick regarded himself as a biblical preacher, although he was as little interested in bringing to the pulpit the intricacies of higher criticism as he was opposed to the literalistic pedestrianism of the fundamentalists. The point, he urged, was to learn how to use Scripture to meet people where they are with a helpful word, in real-life situations. This "is the secret of Christian preaching," he wrote. "We win men to Christianity, not primarily by presenting the involved ideas, but by presenting their incarnation in life. Christ is our great asset. He actually lived the life for which we plead."[6] Fosdick's homiletic and his attitude toward Scripture were shaped not by a commitment to liberal ideas but by his vocation as a pastor and his christocentric ecclesiology, both grounded in the incarnation. Although, as he said, it would not have occurred to him to say the Nicene Creed, still his faith was comprised by "the crux of the matter at which the Nicene Creed was driving.... Christianity is the religion of incarnation and its central affirmation is that God can come into human life."[7] Fosdick's rationalizing of the doctrine is evident even here, but incarnation, and all it means for preaching, remain basic. "Life-situation preaching" is, essentially, a sacramental homiletical idea. If Fosdick had carried his ideas to their fullest implication, then he would have been compelled both by his ecclesiology and his homiletic to give a larger place to the Eucharist.

But his was the situation of the great majority of American preachers. Fosdick contended with an overweening, highly rationalistic fundamentalism, and he did so as a christocentric liberal. We have inherited a great deal from him, and today's continuing movement toward personal and narrative preaching is surely in his debt. In fact, the present emphasis on storytelling may be the end of a movement in American preaching that began with Fosdick, in his struggle to free himself from biblicism. He came to each sermon with real human needs, refusing to traffic in the abstractions of either biblical curiosities or abstruse theology. It is this understanding of preaching, as itself a manifestation of the incarnation, that has taken the field since Fosdick. The full realization of this movement, however, depends—and this may be the emerging movement in homiletics—upon placing preaching more squarely in a sacramental context.

ON THE ROAD

A changing American culture offers considerable impetus for this movement toward preaching as a function of the community's liturgy. An increasingly pluralistic society makes it inevitable that communities will need to find new ways of holding together. Preaching works best, as the center of a congregation's life, when the group is homogeneous. This is especially true of American preaching, in which social and moral questions figure more largely than would be the case in European pulpits. The American preacher is almost bound to express the mores and values of the group, and the more heterogeneous the group the more problematic is preaching. A pulpit-centered church depends upon shared opinion and even similar styles of living. The more pluralistic the society becomes, the more difficult it will be for congregations to cohere around a preacher.

The Homogeneous Audience

One way of coping with this is the drive-in church or the television preacher. The orator skilled at audience analysis and careful to avoid (or to exploit) social, moral, and doctrinal matters can gather an audience of millions around such a common theme as "possibility theology" or, on the negative side, to oppose a common enemy such as "secular humanism," "liberals," or groups or styles that are strange and feared. In either case, the preacher sorts through a vast population made available by the media to find a homogeneous audience, as opposed to a congregation, that can rally to his or her particular message. The result is a network of like-minded people, more often than not alienated from sacramental communities, supporting a preacher who sanctions their commonly held opinions and values.

But in real towns and neighborhoods, where the people who worship together also live together, this is hardly an option. As H. Richard Niebuhr has shown, denominations themselves are a kind of social and economic sorting, and in a more affluent and less pluralistic America, it was possible for people, whether they were immigrants with their own customs and language or simply disgruntled groups, to set themselves up with preachers to suit their needs and tastes.[8] Today, the less expensive and more available voice is the preacher who can be selected by changing channels and supported for a few dollars a month. These personalities—who do not baptize the children of their adherents, do not put the bread in their hands or the wine to their lips, do not join their hands in marriage, and do not stand by their beds or their graves—build their enterprises around speech disconnected from that real human life that becomes, in the mystery of Word and Sacrament, the church.

This disembodied speech is often defended as evangelism, and some of the personalities on television identify with the itinerant preachers who carried the message to the people on the frontier. But this identification needs to be challenged. The frontier preachers traveled months or years on end and brought the gospel to people bodily, preaching in the flesh to families and small communities. The modern preachers who exploit the media will have none of this; in their emphasis upon saving the souls of individuals they do not know, they forgo shaping communities and bodily bringing the gospel to those communities. But is not the deepest meaning of evangelism telling the good news and engrafting men, women, and children into a living body of real people by water, bread, wine, and the Word? Is not the real evangelist the church-in-Christ itself? Any notion of evangelism that does not take the visible body seriously will not only pervert preaching but will, in the long run, weaken its own witness. In this sense, the typical religious orator appearing on the media frustrates the proper work of evangelism, which is to bring people into flesh-and-blood connection with Christ's church. The preacher on television, like the one on the street corner, is not in a position to carry out the work of an evangelist, that is, to connect people with the body of Christ. In short, such preaching is out of place. In spurning the ground on which authentic preaching occurs, it cannot do its proper work, either as kerygma or didache.

Hot Items and Cool Pastors

When Marshall McLuhan, in analyzing media, first put forth his categories of "hot" and "cool" communication, many decided that

preaching was hot.[9] It certainly looked that way, one person standing above the auditors, delivering a one-way monologue, hardly
inviting the kind of participation that McLuhan called "cool." The
efforts to overcome this, such as dialogue sermons, also turned out
to be quite hot. But looking more closely, and taking into account
the system within which the sermon is given, the sermon as a pastoral act turns out to be decidedly cool. The man or woman in the
high pulpit is not just a person giving a speech, but is the one who
lives with these people day to day and plays a crucial role at the
most important transitional events in their experience. That is the
pastor speaking, so that a kind of tacit dialogue is always going on
beneath the monologue. Reuel Howe, in his *Partners in Preaching*,
argues that although the sermon may take the form of a monologue,
it is in fact dialogical in spirit and effect.[10]

This all presupposes that the pastor is the one who should preach.
Good liturgical practice, for example, suggests that when the sermon occurs at the Eucharist, the celebrant should be the preacher.
Because preaching is the culmination of a pastoral dialogue, constant conversation needs to occur in the congregation. The sermon,
when it falls away from its connection with the community, lapses
into the intellectualism, moralism, emotionalism, promotionalism,
and entertainment that characterize much pulpiteering in America. Losing connection with the pastoral element, it takes on the
unfortunate characteristics of a media event.

The irony is that the television personalities cultivate a "cool"
style. The most obvious example is the preacher as talk-show host.
Most of these figures have learned the techniques of involving the
audience, from taking a mobile microphone down the center aisle to
cultivating a peripatetic style. (Norman Vincent Peale was a pioneer
of this homiletical style, preaching without a pulpit and cultivating
an engaging folksiness. It is no surprise that Robert Schuller was a
protégé of the great communicator of Fifth Avenue's Marble Colle-
giate Church.) The accompanying music tends to ape the popular,
and camera and sets aim at up-close, intimate engagement. Assessed
as a communication technique, a comfortable environment is created, inviting the audience in. Thus, what homiletics teachers have
been urging upon their students since Fosdick is realized: conversational communication. Television lends itself to this cool style

remarkably well, so that even a religious message can be sold to millions.

But if talk-show style is put in the context of ecclesiology, then it must be described in different terms. If the presupposition of this book is accepted, that preaching is a function of the body of Christ, and that this body is identified by reference to Word and Sacrament, then the kind of participation that makes preaching truly cool is not only absent in television but also frustrated. The speech of the pulpit is cool first of all because it occurs in the context of a community connected prior to the event, and secondarily because the preacher is disclosing a reality known by sacramental participation. What is crucial here, in any critique of religious life in America today, is that this reality, the presence of Christ to his people, is a matter of flesh and blood. It is in this context that authentic preaching occurs, the numerical and financial success of the "televangelists" notwithstanding.

Itinerant and Electronic

So when Brilioth describes "freedom from liturgical fetters" as the most common characteristic of American preaching, he points to the historical, sociological, and ecclesiological sources of the present homiletical situation. On the front lawn of the seminary in which I teach is a heroic equestrian statue of Francis Asbury, a great Methodist circuit rider. Bible under his arm, the itinerant preacher carries the message to one meeting after another on the frontier. The United Methodist Church follows to this day a modified form of this system of itineracy. Although pastors presently remain with a given congregation for longer than four years, this brief tenure was at one time almost the rule. Even today, however, pastors are moved from one charge to another with relative frequency. A model that was appropriate for an unchurched America is being perpetuated, not only among United Methodists but among most denominations, in a society that, although highly mobile, is far removed from the unsettled frontier.

For a good part of my life I have been an itinerant preacher, serving in my primary vocation as a professor and at the same time preaching far and wide. This varied from the short-term interim— in which I gave the sermons while other members of the staff took care of people in the hospital, crises in families, and even weddings and funerals—to the different pulpit each Sunday. For several years one affluent church flew me in for a summer Sunday: dinner, a bed and breakfast in a hotel, to the church to give the sermon, lunch with one of the congregation's leaders, and back on the plane to Newark. Similar to that hit-and-run style, there is even a circuit of endowed "preacherships" in the United States and Canada, quite large trusts for the sole purpose of bringing star preachers for brief series of sermons in the great pulpits.

A very high estimate of the place and importance of preaching in the life of the church might seem to lie behind such generous provision for preaching: People are willing to spend money on the pulpit! Moreover, practical arguments can be made for an itinerant vocation in preaching. Are there not those among us who have a special message to bring, or a special gift for bringing it that should be shared widely in the church? Cannot the itinerant bring a different perspective, prophetic insight, and new knowledge to a provincial parish? Further, when and where would bishops, denominational leaders, and seminary professors preach if the validity of itinerant preaching were denied?

At the same time, those who do this kind of preaching would be the first to acknowledge that it is not deeply satisfying. This is true even of many seminary chapels, where the congregation is itself transient, and where the realities of academic life inhibit the development of close relationships like those between pastor and congregation. For both of these reasons, the chapels of academic institutions are often problematic for preaching, and they can frequently foster the disembodiment of the Word. Anyone who has had the experience of preaching as a pastor and as a peripatetic will know the difference, and will understand something of the problem of the disembodied Word.

Is it a preacher who ministers or a minister who preaches? Putting the question this way is itself misleading, suggesting that these two can be split apart so easily. But in fact they are, both in popular perception and in actual practice. Richard Baxter has articulated the close connection between pastor and preacher.[11] But one can still hear the pastor referred to as "the preacher," and it is the case that most congregations seeking a new minister place the ability

to preach at the top of the job description. This one activity is sin-
gled out for emphasis, given special rewards, and in extreme cases
allowed to usurp the pastoral office. To assert that it is the minister, specifically the pastor, who preaches would imply a reversal of
values and attitudes in many congregations, and among many pastors. It would suggest a much more holistic theology of ministry
than is current in the church. Just such a theology, however, puts
preaching in its proper place.

But does not this call into question the nonparochial preaching
of some of the greatest homileticians of our time? What about the
voices on radio during the middle decades of this century, Harry
Emerson Fosdick, an ecumenical Baptist, and Edmund A. Steimle, a
Lutheran? Those men, along with such nationally known preachers
as Norman Vincent Peale, Fulton J. Sheen, and Ralph W. Sockman,
spoke to millions every week. People actually got up early on Sunday morning to tune in a preacher before going to church. There
lies the crucial difference: The people who listened to these preachers were, by and large, active members of congregations, and the
preachers in the tone and content of their preaching reinforced
their hearers in that affiliation. These preachers presupposed that
they were preaching to baptized, communing Christians. Edmund
Steimle's style, to take one example, was, both in content and delivery, attentive to a more secular way of thinking about the faith,
but he spoke as a preacher of the church to people who knew what
it was to live in the church, people who had been baptized and
went to Communion. In short, the great radio preachers themselves knew the pastoral situation—all of them had considerable
experience as settled pastors—and it was out of that experience
that they preached. Even the titles of the programs tell us as much:
"The National Radio Pulpit" and "The Protestant Hour." The format of these broadcasts included basic liturgical elements familiar
to churchgoers. In the case of "The Protestant Hour," the format
was very like what happened in church on Sunday morning, in the
reading of Scripture, the music, the prayers, and the sermon. The
preacher of the day could be easily identified with one's own pastor
and the sermon with that in one's own church.

At the same time, the move toward the media must have made,
in the long run, its own contribution to the disembodiment of the

Word. Inevitably, people compared their minister, as preacher, with these giants, and so long as the comparison stopped with sermonic ability, most local pastors did not come off too well. Moreover, with these preachers a new possibility became clear: One could relate to a religious personality, even participate in a religious organization, without going to church. If it is true that the first big step toward the vaporization of American religion began with the antisacramentalism of Emerson, then the second was the rise of revivalism: Although its initial effect was to bring multitudes into the churches, revivalism raised up the religious leader, often a reformer with a moral cause, as independent from the church. And the third step was the media-preacher phenomenon of our own time. All have made their contribution to the present situation: Religion continues to be a major ingredient of American life; there are preachers on every hand; and the churches continue to decline in membership and influence.

THE DISEMBODIED WORD

The pathology of the disembodied Word should be apparent to the reader. Quite apart from the misleading and even perverse use of preaching by those who exploit the media, one can see within the churches themselves what happens when Word and Sacrament are split apart and sermons originate from sources other than intentional, participatory life in Christ. Although these are generalizations, here are five symptoms of the disembodied Word, preaching occurring as something other than a function of the sacramental community.

Congregation as Audience

One of my students, speaking of the difficulty of preaching, spoke of his congregation as "those people out there." Perceived in that way, the congregation becomes employer, resistant customer, judge and jury, even adversary. It is virtually a given in our culture that sermons will become one more commodity to be consumed and churchgoers will approach the sermon as they would other goods and services: Is it "good" or "bad"? Does it meet my needs? Is it attractive? Does it make me feel good? And this, in the worst case, propels the preacher into a performance motivated unduly by ego and into a situation that sometimes leads to debilitating stress.

When I first began to preach, as a very young man, my biggest problem was sweating, which was associated with my peculiar habit of standing on my toes through the entire sermon. I might as well have been a ballet dancer for the heroic effort that preaching called forth. Years later, I was led to reflect on that college-days experience when I came across Dietrich Bonhoeffer's lectures on homiletics to the students at Finkenwald, a small seminary of the Confessing Church. Bonhoeffer said that if the preacher manifests extraordinary physical symptoms, then we should ask questions about that person's theology and spiritual formation.[12] I realized then that in my college days I had been performing for an audience rather than preaching to a congregation.

For his part, Bonhoeffer would not even conduct sermon "labs," because he believed that sermons could be given and heard only in a truly worshiping congregation. The preacher cannot preach and the congregation cannot hear in a situation defined by an audience. What is the posture and attitude in which one hears the Word of God? Arms folded across the chest, as if to say, "Okay preacher, now give me a sermon"? Or is it more the posture of prayer, in the common humility of faith seeking understanding? What is the difference between an audience and a congregation?

The Preacher in the Spotlight

The parish in which I serve has a new lighting system, and it is just the thing a fine old church needs. The lighting alone, illumining the altar and choir, has brought us all closer together in worship. We also have a spotlight on the pulpit and rheostats in the nave, an arrangement more and more common in our churches. The spotlight goes up on the preacher as the congregation recedes into dusky spectatorship. Some see in this the power of the movies, the intensity of communication promoted by the anonymity of the darkened house and a one-to-one engagement between the preacher and each listener. There may be something to this, although even it smacks of an individualistic piety being served by the sermon. Whatever else we may make of it, spotlighting the preacher and rendering the congregation passive (they cannot even contribute facial expression!) reflect the understanding of preaching that pervades our churches: The congregation is an audience and the preacher a performer. Small wonder that sleeplessness and indigestion mark many preachers' Saturday nights and Sunday mornings. Again, Bonhoeffer would have us ask theological questions about such arrangements, and such symptoms.

Sacraments in the Shadows

The sermon's overshadowing of the sacraments is not just a matter of the infrequency of Holy Communion by comparison to the weekly fare of preaching; it also has to do with the fact that most sermons largely ignore the sacraments. What are we to make, for example, of the "communion meditation"? The usual explanation is that the sermon must be shortened to accommodate the additional ritual. But does not this language suggest the distance we feel between preaching and Sacrament and, in yet one more way, push the Sacrament aside? It is not unusual to hear people defend occasional Communion on the grounds that it makes the rite "more special," as if that were a virtue in Christian liturgy. There can be no doubt that separating Word from Sacrament has the effect of displacing the table from the center of the church's life.

This is symbolized in many ways. Those churches that have a sermon every Sunday and "observe" the Lord's Supper once a quarter are obvious examples. But even in churches with more frequent observance, it is not unusual to see the Holy Communion tacked on to a preaching service, so that the pressure of time is felt where one wishes least to be rushed, at a meal. This is often the case with Baptism as well: Neither the worship nor the sermon is oriented to the Sacrament. Rather, the Sacrament is one more item in the usual preaching hour. The powerful visual symbols are present: the table given over to holding the Bible, flowers, offering plates— everything but the bread and wine. Often the relative size of the table and its placement in relation to the pulpit tell us at a glance what is preeminent here.

St. Peter's Lutheran Church in New York City is a most satisfying environment for Christian liturgy. The architect has achieved a balance of Word and Sacrament in materials, colors, and arrangement. One enters the church near a large baptismal pool, where running water is a steady reminder of how each person comes into Christ's body. The three other essential furnishings—presiding chairs, pulpit, and table—are constructed on a similar scale of equally good materials, and they are placed as a harmonious trio, the table at the center balanced by the pulpit, which stands closer to the congregation. The three chairs are themselves powerful symbols of the continuity of the church and the presence of Christ the host in both Word and Sacrament.

The Bible as Mystery

In a way that closely parallels making the Eucharist so special that we would not want to celebrate it in the community very often, the disembodied Word leads to a notion of Scripture as mystery. The book itself is referred to as the Holy Bible, treated with the respect a more catholic community would give to the consecrated bread and wine, and even given an exalted place on the altar—sometimes in the place, incidentally, in which some high churches would keep the reserved Sacrament. A well-known hymn prays, "Break thou the bread of life, dear Lord, to me," as a reference not to the eucharistic blessing and breaking of bread but to the Bible. Here we have a biblical piety in which texts of Scripture become sacramental, carrying the presence of Christ, a devotion on which a great many Christians have lived their lives. Today the Bible-study group, meeting to share with each other sacred texts, is as close as many people come to those early groups of Christians who met regularly for the "breaking of bread and prayers." It is out of this piety that the typical North American sermon has come, based on a small piece of Scripture and aimed at being practically edifying and emotionally compelling.[13]

In the context of an anti-Roman bias following the Reformation, it was inevitable that the Bible would become the holy mystery and the preacher the dispenser of its sacred elements. This has led to many abuses. One of the most ironic is the reduction of the Bible to a collection of curiosities, in much the same way that the medieval mind regarded the consecrated bread and wine as magical in themselves. Similarly, meticulous preoccupation with isolated verses and the ascription of authority to disconnected pericopes are analogous to the most pious adoration of bread and wine in isolation from the community's celebration of the sacramental presence of Christ. Although few who use the Bible in this way would put it in those terms, nevertheless texts of Scripture are wrested from context, elaborated in the most amazing ways, and raised to the level of icons worthy of endless contemplation. The present neo-apocalypticism and nit-picking biblicism have come into being with the disembodiment of the Word, the substitution among many Protestants of the Bible for the mystery of Christ's presence in Word and Sacrament.

The Abandoned Pulpit

A cartoon in *The New Yorker* shows a preacher in one of those open, wrought-iron pulpits, like the one in Manhattan's Madison Avenue Presbyterian Church. The preacher, visible head to toe, is highly exercised. In one of the front pews, a child is bending to his mother and saying: "Mommy, what will he do if he gets out of there?!"

The media aside, we are hearing—one might even say *seeing*—more and more sermons delivered from outside the pulpit. The lavaliere (a little microphone named for a jeweled pendant favored by the Duchesse de La Vallière, mistress of Louis XIV) has made it possible to preach on the steps, in the aisle, on the move, even at the table or font. Increasingly pulpits stand empty as the preacher goes wandering. This practice, both in parish churches and at seminaries, gets mixed reviews.

The practice of moving outside the pulpit does address several concerns of homiletical communication: to give a clear signal that the preacher wants to communicate; to be able to read the body language and facial expressions of the people better, by being closer; to appear informal. Some preachers say that they feel free outside the pulpit, better able to express themselves extemporaneously. Also, moving away from the pulpit recognizes, if tacitly, the changing styles of authority that the clergy exercise in the church. The pulpit, often elevated and imposing, may suggest an outmoded authoritarianism that the preacher, especially, seeks to avoid.

These seem quite valid, even persuasive reasons for leaving the pulpit. But the question of symbolic communication should also be raised: What does the pulpit itself symbolize for the congregation, and what does leaving it actually say? Within the context of this inquiry into the Word as embodiment, this becomes an important question. Can there be any doubt that in many congregations the pulpit symbolizes the community's trusteeship of preaching and the present preacher's continuity with all those who have gone before? Preaching in a historic Presbyterian church in which nothing but the congregation has changed since 1843, I found myself moved, and empowered, by the venerable pulpit itself, by the sense of continuity with many preachers and congregations. Is the pulpit, at least potentially, a concrete symbol of the ongoing life of the people of God in this particular place, which is the source and aim of each sermon? Does the pulpit guard the congregation, and the preacher, from the notion that the sermon is this particular preacher's doing and from the debilitating idea that each sermon is created *de novo*, as if many others had not stood here and, indeed, preached on this very text? It may be that not only the table, but also the actual presence of the pulpit, help to keep the preacher in place. The pulpit ought not to be abandoned without reflecting on these questions, for preaching is not first of all a matter of communication, but of communion.

In the situation of the disembodied Word, which is very largely the condition of contemporary North American Protestantism, the trends named above—for example, the spotlighted preacher using Scripture to rouse and edify a passive audience, and the audience being increasingly distanced from the sacraments and what Brilioth called "the great fact of salvation in the history of revelation"— frequently issue in worship as entertainment. This is just the point at which the media preachers take over because the church is hardly in a position to compete with the technique, money, and talent available to these preachers and their organizations. The seminaries, for a time, imagined equipping studios and training students to imitate the radio and television preachers, an enterprise now largely abandoned, not only because they lacked funds and personnel but also because we have come to see that we are about a different kind of ministry altogether. Entertainment sells on the media; the liturgical and homiletical practices of the American churches have played into the hands of those who sell religion. The people who respond to the media preachers have learned worship as entertainment in the churches of cities and towns across the land.

Most human beings, allowed healthy development and maturing, have a decreasing need for entertainment—passive consumption—and move toward active creativity. That is one reason we are seeing communities of faith turning from the disembodied Word and struggling to find ways to act out in Word and Sacrament the presence of Christ among us.

3
Preaching as a Liturgical Act

Let the word of Christ dwell in you richly, teach and admonish one another in all wisdom, and sing psalms and hymns and spiritual songs with thankfulness in your hearts to God. And whatever you do, in word or deed, do everything in the name of the Lord Jesus, giving thanks to God the Father through him.
—Col. 3:16-17

The source of the preached word is not the pious Christian experience or consciousness of the preacher, nor the need of the hour of the congregation, nor the desire to improve or influence others. All of these things quickly collapse and lead to resignation. These motivations and forces are not enough. The only valid source of the sermon is the commission of Christ to proclaim the gospel, and also the knowledge that this commission comes to us from an already existing church. The source of the sermon is nothing other than the existence of the church of Christ.
—Dietrich Bonhoeffer,
"The Causality and Finality of Preaching"

I arrived at the church early on Easter Day, the sermon well in hand for the three services of the morning. The day's homily would begin with the familiar narrative from Luke and lead the congregation to the Easter acclamation. While scanning my typescript one last time (because I would not take it to the pulpit), the door opened and the lay reader greeted me, "The Lord is risen!"

That started me thinking afresh about the role of the preacher in worship. Before I stood up to preach, or had even put on my vestments, the liturgy of Easter was beginning, with this layperson and among the people who were dressing their children, sharing a festive breakfast, and making their way to the church. Whatever I might have to say today would be but one voice—a crucial one to be

sure—among the many voices who in song and prayer, the words
of the Eucharist and the babble at the social hour, would be saying
"Christ is risen!" Was my role to convince anyone of the truth of
Easter, or even to give a great sermon for such a great day? The
layperson's greeting that morning tipped me off to a quite different
task, to make one vital contribution to the morning's liturgy. The
sermon might, in this way of seeing it, not so much initiate the
Easter acclamation as echo it.

KNOWING OUR PLACE

Anyone who has preached on one of the great feast days knows
that it is not the time for the great sermon: The best rule, in fact, is
the bigger the occasion, the smaller the sermon. Also, the task is not
to be novel, even original, but to tell the familiar stories in much
the same way that a family, gathered for a reunion, marriage, or
burial, tells the well-worn tales. Especially at Christmas and Easter,
the weight of the event and the power of the familiar liturgy—
its treasured propers, prayers, and music—and the congregation's
ownership of these occasions put the preacher in his or her proper
place, as a companion to the liturgy. That is exactly the way I would
describe what hit me that Easter morning in the vestry, that my
preaching was *among* those who came gratefully to break bread.
Such moments *put us in our place*—a positive, liberating phrase—
reminding us that people do not come to church to listen to the
preacher, not ultimately, but to hear echoed from the pulpit their
own voices. Can there be any doubt that we preach best when we
are able to say in the pulpit what the men and women, girls and boys
sitting before us would say if they had the chance and could find the
words? Though I ended my sermon that Easter morning with "The
Lord is risen!" and the congregation responded with "He is risen
indeed!" reflection on the place of the preacher in liturgy might
lead us to reverse those roles.

Liturgy Forming Sermon

For the first time, in Atlanta in 1982, the Academy of Homiletics and the North American Academy of Liturgy—associations
of university and seminary professors in Canada and the United
States—met together. A difficult meeting, it reflected the distance

between sermon and liturgy in many of our churches. A remarkably productive meeting, we struggled with the question of the place of preaching in worship. For example, those who planned the services of worship in the chapel at Emory University framed both the reading of the lessons and the sermon with silence. After the reading of the Gospel and before the sermon, silence; when the preacher sat down, silence. That simple change in our usual practice—silence for many of us is liturgical innovation!—had an immediate, discernible impact on the sermons. As the week moved along, the content, tone, style, and mood of preaching were altered. The homileticians' fears were confirmed: More attention to liturgy might well change the way we preach.

Garrison Keillor, the storyteller of "A Prairie Home Companion," when asked what sermons should sound like, answered the question in liturgical terms: "When a minister stands in front of people he is interrupting what the people have come to church for. He had better have a good reason for doing that. . . . We go [to church] to look at the mysteries, and all the substitutes for communion with God are not worth anyone's time."[1]

Most of us who preach assume—and this is true to our heritage in the Reformation—that talking and communion with God are not mutually exclusive. Yet, if we become preoccupied with talking, especially the preacher's talking, we might forget the real business of Sunday morning, which is probably closer to "the mysteries," in which preaching, when sensitively and appropriately done, is pivotal. The worst that can happen—and preachers especially suffer when this occurs in a congregation—is a preoccupation with preaching that leads to liturgical passivity. One of the most promising aspects of liturgical renewal is that people who take up their own role in worship will be more responsive, more involved in the sermon, rather than sitting like the passive consumer of television shows expecting to be entertained by a performance. Liturgical renewal that leads people to sing and pray, to share the peace of Christ and come together in a celebrative Eucharist, to do their proper and most important work, can only be a boon to preaching. Active worshipers will be, to use Chester Pennington's phrase, "talented listeners."[2] So every move we make to return worship to the people advances the cause of preaching.

Since Vatican II, liturgical styles have moved toward simplicity. Minimalism in church architecture, especially in Europe, expresses the liturgical reforms that seek to recover what is essential in Christian worship. Unadorned spaces, openness, light, the earthiness of natural materials, and buildings on a human scale suggest a liturgical sensibility that is increasingly chaste and understated. Paralleling that in liturgy is a return to the simple symmetry of the service of Word and table, to congregational presentation of music, Scripture, and prayer, and to silence. How shall preaching take its place in this movement toward simplicity, "congregationalism," and the normative service of Word and table?

Back to Scripture

Take one example of liturgical change and its implications for preaching, the place of Scripture in worship. Vatican II declared that Christ "is present in His word, since it is He Himself who speaks when the holy Scriptures are read in the church."[3] This means that Scripture merits time in the service, careful preparation of the lay readers, silence following the reading, and the liturgical regularity of following the lectionary and reading all the lessons. It also means that introductions and explanations, pious interjections and mini-exegeses are not just superfluous but could even prevent the hearer from apprehending Christ's presence in the unadorned words of Scripture itself.

This also means that the Scriptures may mediate Christ's presence before the preacher stands up. Accordingly, such liturgical scholars as James White tell us that the lections have their own life in the ongoing life of the congregation and should be read faithfully whether or not they are preached upon. (Even the practice of trying to touch upon all the lessons in the sermon, which seldom works well, suggests that the efficacy of Scripture lies in preaching.) What we have is a liturgical act—which may be either as simple as a person standing up in the congregation to read or as elaborate as a gospel procession—in which someone reads the Bible aloud, without comment, while the people listen and find in this, as Vatican II suggests, the "real presence" of Christ.

It is this simple act, remarkably enough, that is probably most common to the worship of all Christians (Catholic, Orthodox, Protestant), and much more is being made of it now. In the ecumenical community of Taizé, for example, the reading of Scripture occupies a special place at worship, morning, noon, and evening. The reading is done in an unusual place, from a lectern at the rear of the church, so that one hears while contemplating the beautiful icons, the communion table, and the wall of candles at the front of the church. The Scriptures are also read in several languages, by the clear voices of people well prepared for what is, unmistakably, a holy task. This is the Word at weekday prayers—the only sermon is on Sunday morning—though there are Bible-study groups each morning after breakfast. This experience of hearing the Bible read in worship, without comment, is instructive for anyone trying to understand the pronouncement of Vatican II that here Christ is fully present, and especially for those of us who have related to Scripture primarily through the preacher who takes a text and sets that, sometimes only a snippet, at the center of worship.

We are moving toward locating preaching in liturgy. For a beginning, the revivalist order of service, which puts the sermon at the end and tends to reduce everything else to build-up, is giving way to a eucharistic pattern, even where weekly Eucharist is not the rule. The increasing use of the lectionary, too, locates preaching liturgically: The preacher speaks as one who, like the congregation, listens to the common texts. These shifts, away from locating the sermon at the apex of worship, and toward a commonly held biblical corpus, have given many preachers the sense of preaching *in* the liturgy, even of being carried by it.

But there remains a considerable lag between what we know about the history and nature of Christian worship and what occurs on Sunday morning. The earliest accounts of the church's life show us people meeting to eat and drink, to pray and sing, and in this context to read Scripture and hear from the presbyter. This "dwelling in Christ richly" was around a table, and we have images—in Justin Martyr, for example, about A.D. 150—of the "president" of the Eucharist preaching at the table.[4] This image, of the close relationship of Word and table, is gradually reshaping our worship. The consequences for preaching are far-reaching.

Karl Barth defined proclamation by such an image: "By 'proclamation of the Word of God' we are to understand withal, primarily and decisively, preaching and the sacraments."[5] By this definition, preaching would be at every point, in its inception, preparation, and delivery—whatever its distinguishing characteristics and however much it may depend upon the preacher's person and craft—a function of the community of the baptized gathered around the holy table. Even the content of the sermon, its language coming from this very community, is analogous to the sacraments. Like bread, wine, and water, the words and idiom, stories and images of the very time and place become, in the sermon, the gifts of God for the people of God.

Barth, like virtually all the Reformers before him, believed that the proper place for preaching is at the table. That is to say, there is no place in which preaching is so enabled or validated as in the presence of the sacraments, and some would go so far as to say that apart from the sacramental community there is no reason to preach. Preaching belongs to the church—an obvious truth, easily forgotten—the signs of whose belonging to Christ are Baptism and Eucharist. Commenting on Barth's theology of proclamation, Dietrich Ritschl writes: "The sermon and the Lord's Supper are not 'contradistinguished,' but it is the one life-giving Word that is present in both. The presence of the risen Lord and the expectation of His return are the decisive elements in the sermon and the Lord's Supper: We bear in mind both when we say 'proclamation.'"[6]

The preacher who keeps close to the table is more likely to keep to the specific task that the church is about, to remember why and what we preach. The sacraments, in all their materiality, hold us to the gospel, to Christ: "*Ho logos sarx egeneto* (John 1:14)—preaching, too, can and must say this. But in a way which preaching can never do, the sacrament underlines *sarx* and *egeneto*."[7] The preacher who keeps the baptistry in view—another good reason for placing it at the entrance, in full view—will be more likely to remember that it is God who calls, saves, forgives, leads, and sustains these people, and that quite apart from the issue of the sermon, these people have been grafted into Christ by Baptism. Preaching on Rev. 7:9-17, Jon Walton asks his congregation, "Who are these, clothed in white . . . , who approach the throne of the Lamb?" He concludes his sermon in a way that reveals where his eye, and his question, have landed: "I ask you, you who have been baptized in Christ, how far from the throne do you think we are? No farther than from here to . . . , say, that baptismal font?"[8] That sermon could just have well gone off into speculations or moralistic exhortation. But the preacher cannot forget that the congregants are the baptized in Christ. They have been washed, and it is the preacher's role to assure them of this and then to tell them what that means for living in this world.

The sermon at the font will not be moralistic, just as preaching before the table will not take a tone that suggests that God's love is somehow conditional, for all are invited by Christ himself. From baptistry to table, by way of Scripture and an encounter, in the sermon, of the way it is with us in this place here and now, the people are moving toward the moment when, once more, Jesus will eat with sinners. This is the place, at the table, where gospel preaching is most assured, and the preacher who stands there with the baptistry in full view will be more inclined to give thanks than to complain, to bless than to curse. Is this not the only really safe place to preach the law, in the presence of Christ who finally says to all, "Come . . . "?

Much preaching in America is literally out of place and has lost its underpinnings. The legacy of the Reformation, although it would come as a shock to the Reformers, is schism between preaching and the sacramental community. Taking the place of the sometimes atrophied, often exploited Mass, and to carry out the program of the new movements, the sermon assumed a very large place in the Protestant ethos, just as the men who preached took on proportions larger than life. This has continued to the present and has been reinforced by the revivalist movement, individualism, our susceptibility to the huckster, our practical bent, and the media that lend themselves to a particular type of preacher. Moreover, for many Americans, the bottom line is success, numerical and fiscal.

That preaching has been separated from its proper context is revealed especially by the "electronic church," and increasingly in the use of the Bible and sermon by various groups lobbying for one cause or another. At times it has even seemed possible that a religio-political coalition, with a narrowly focused platform amounting to a value-specific agenda, could gain political power by the use of a kind of preaching. To what degree would responsibility for that lie with our willingness, now well established, to accept as preaching religiously oriented speech, somehow related to the Bible, outside the sacramental community? To what degree has preaching, loosed from its sacramental moorings, been commandeered by culture-religion? Is it not the case that in America anyone can stand up anytime and anyplace, quote the Bible, and be a preacher? Are we willing to perpetuate that idea? The question comes down to specific practice if we ask: Do we give tacit approval to such an idea when the sermon, in our own worship, occurs independently of the sacraments?

Placing preaching firmly in the liturgy is more likely to keep us close to the gospel and away from chauvinism, moralism, parochialism, and the unworthy agendas that crowd in upon us. Keeping preaching close to sacrament is the best way to prevent its perversion, as William Skudlarek tells us:

> Worship, or liturgy, or sacrament, then, is something far more than the setting of the sermon. It is even more than the kairos of preaching. . . . It is, to use that old but at times still helpful category of scholastic philosophy, the "final cause" of preaching: its end, purpose, and goal. To say this is not to deny that preaching is to bring people to faith, or that it is to have an influence on their behavior. Rather, it is to affirm that faith and obedience are to go one step further and be transformed into praise and thanksgiving. Unless this step is taken faith can all too easily degenerate into doctrinal rigidity, and obedience into legalistic conformity. Authentic praise and thanksgiving—that is, praise and thanksgiving flowing out of a recognition of the graciousness of God (faith) and propelling us to actions of love and justice (obedience)—is ultimately the mark of effective proclamation of the word of God.[9]

Paul, in his letter to the Colossians, admonishes the church to let Christ's word dwell in us "richly." Authentic preaching takes its place in, and makes its contribution to, this communal richness.

PREACHER AND PRIEST

Such placement of the sermon suggests that preaching is a much more priestly function than we may have recognized. The preacher has most often been identified with the scholar, the prophet, the teacher, and the evangelist, sometimes more closely linked even with the administrator and promoter than with the priest. But if preaching is in fact a function of the sacramental community, then is it not in his or her priestly capacity that the pastor preaches?

Priest as Pastor

In the church to which I belong, it is customary for the priest to drink whatever remains in the cup at the end of the Eucharist. At the *ablutions*, as this clearing of the table is called, the one presiding and those assisting drink the last of the wine, water is poured into the chalice, and the priest drinks the dregs. Although there is no intentional symbolism in this manner of disposing of the eucharistic wine—it is simply washing up after a meal—in this act the priest makes a physical connection with every person who has drunk from the cup and, in effect, with the entire congregation. In the early years of the AIDS epidemic some communicants were declining the cup. A bishop in California announced that he would drain the cup at the end of each Eucharist, as an appropriate pastoral act. In this simple action, whether it is a bishop showing solidarity with a troubled diocese or the pastor presiding week after week, there emerges a powerful symbol of corporate life in Christ and of the bonding between pastor and people. Here is the one who preaches: the one whose life is deeply connected with these people, the one who in the holy meal drinks with them the cup of mingled joy and sorrow, all leading to great thanksgiving. Anyone who has had this priestly experience will know the truth of this deep bonding, just as anyone who has preached out of the depths of a congregation's life will understand the sense in which preaching is a priestly vocation.

Priest as Prophet

This embodiment, the close identification of the life of a community of faith with one person—so clearly seen when an individual stands at the altar on behalf of all—is essential to all the pastoral offices, including that of the prophet. Walter Brueggemann, perhaps more helpfully than anyone, has described the prophetic function as creating "an alternate consciousness": "The task of prophetic ministry is to nurture, nourish, and evoke a consciousness and perception alternative to the consciousness and perception of the dominant culture around us."[10] This is accomplished, Brueggemann says, in two acts: dismantling and energizing. "The dismantling begins in the groans and laments of the people; the energizing begins in the doxologies of the new community."[11] The prophet is

the one who brings to expression what afflicts the community—
including its sins—and, at the same time, evokes the vision of a
new possibility.

This figure necessarily comprises, along with the specific function of the prophet, the roles of pastor and priest. Brueggemann's
language sketches the profile of the Eucharist where—in the narratives of creation and fall, the broken covenant with Israel, the
suffering and death of Jesus—the human condition is rehearsed
and, at the same time, transcended in the celebration of the presence of the risen Christ. The Eucharist is, in Brueggemann's model,
a prophetic act that combines the dismantling of the structures of
power that defy God and oppress goodness with the energizing
presence of the one for whose coming all things wait. The priest
at the altar, no less than the preacher in the pulpit, is at work
dismantling and energizing.

Jeremiah provides a good example of this embodied prophetic
Word. At a low point in his career, Jeremiah is *persona non grata*
in his home town of Anathoth and, because of his pessimistic estimate of the state of the nation, under house arrest in Jerusalem.
The armies of Babylon are besieging the city, and Jeremiah is pre-
dicting imminent defeat for King Zedekiah. In the midst of this dire
situation, Jeremiah's cousin Hanamel urges upon him familial duty,
to buy some ancestral land at Anathoth. At a time when the value of
real estate is plummeting, Jeremiah puts down seventeen shekels
of silver and signs the deed before witnesses. Then he reveals, in
one of his dramatic actions, the mind of the prophet: "Take these
deeds . . . and put them in an earthenware vessel, that they may last
for a long time. For thus says the Lord of hosts, the God of Israel:
Houses and fields and vineyards shall again be bought in this land"
(Jer. 32:14b-15).

Then Jeremiah tells, once more, the story of Israel, its deliverance
from slavery in Egypt into "a land flowing with milk and honey,"
its disobedience and subsequent desolation. But, he continues, the
word comes to him: "Buy the land . . . though the city is given into
the hands of the Chaldeans" (32:25). The city will go up in smoke
and the people into exile, but the day of return will come, "and I
will plant them in this land in faithfulness, with all my heart and
soul" (32:41).

Here is the prophet, dismantling the prevailing consciousness, but always keeping both the past and the future in view. Jeremiah speaks out of the story that has brought Israel to its predicament, but he sees the end of the story not in the present but in a splendid future. Here is also the pastor, who belongs to the people—like it or not!—and has a stake in their future. And here is the priest—in the way that we presently understand that office—vested by memory and imagination in the history and future of the community and articulating that by word and gesture. In this single figure, the roles of prophet, priest, and pastor coalesce. This can be seen, also, in such an ironic figure as Graham Greene's whiskey priest, who embodies the historical and social situation of a people and at his packing-case Mass brings a foretaste—as does every Eucharist—of that heavenly city toward which he and his people yearn.[12] Here is a person who embodies, despite his all-too-obvious failings, the historical and social situation of a community and the vision that moves it toward the future. How would one sort out pastor, priest, and prophet? Only a pastor, with a stake in the people's lives, one who will go into exile with them, has credibility as a prophet. Only the priest, whose words and gestures come from a people's memory and vision, can speak the Word that is both realistic and life-giving.

Prophet, Priest, and Pastor

The Cathedral of San Fernando is on the main plaza in the old city of San Antonio. Father Virgilio Elizondo is the priest in charge, in a parish with a large number of displaced persons, many of whom, as "illegals," have great difficulty finding employment, housing, and medical care. We went to a folk Mass on Thursday night in the spacious old church made more beautiful by the simplicity that Vatican II has brought. There had been some question as we approached the church: Would we be "welcome to receive"? As the service unfolded, that question receded far into the background, pushed aside by the weight of real human struggle and the hunger for Communion whetted by the prophetic situation.

A mariachi band—men, women, and teenagers who, we learned later, had skipped supper to play for the Mass—was ranged behind the table. The pastor arrived late, putting on his alb as he made his way through the band to stand behind the table, free-standing at the crossing. He greeted us, asked if we could worship without a bulletin, and explained that he had been delayed at the hospital with a sixteen-year-old boy who had lost a leg. With this he called the motley congregation—Spanish-speaking persons, Anglos, professional people, and rough-handed laborers, old and young—to the eucharistic celebration, to bless the Lord.

In the sermon that evening, the pastor told the story of his parish and of the boy in the hospital. The teenager, riding boxcars out of Mexico, had got his leg caught in a coupling. The priest told this story not as if it were sensational, or even extraordinary, but as a part of one more day in the life of his people, what Edmund Steimle would have called "the fabric" of their lives.[13] This was not a sermon illustration, but a common story belonging to the whole community, shared in this moment of preaching like broken bread and the wine of Jesus' own suffering. The pastor spoke of the recent visit of John Paul II, with appreciation and affection, but went on to say that his people could not spend their energy on the issues that preoccupy the highest leaders of the church: Their mission was clear and preoccupying, to take care of the homeless, unemployed, and needy people who thronged the cathedral and passed through its shadow. He went on to tell us that his parish has the heaviest offering in Texas, "not the biggest, but definitely the heaviest." In the quiet laughter there was the unmistakable confidence and deep joy of people hearing a believable human voice speaking of their real situation and, at the same time, calling them to give thanks and rejoice in Christ.

Here was a priest preaching, a pastor and prophet, moving between the common life that he embodied and the eucharistic table around which the community wept and prayed and sang. The sermon moved through the story of that Thursday to Scripture and prayer and, finally, to the altar. There was about it a sense of reality, of the merging of politics and piety, which was as palpable as the calluses of the hand that took mine at the Peace. Though the people around us spoke no English and the differences between us were all too obvious, here once more, in Word and Sacrament, the body of Christ was joined. It would have been impossible that evening to draw a line between pastor and priest, between priest and preacher. They all combined in this earnest, joyful man who enabled that community to face the world and who put into the words of prayer and preaching its "laments and groans," in such a way that all were brought finally to lift up our hearts in mariachi music and ancient liturgy.

This integration of Word, Sacrament, and common life is missing from the experience of many Christians in North America. The pastor without the prophet too easily becomes the socially scrupulous chaplain to a complacently homogeneous club. The priest without the prophet loses the connection between the drama of the crucifixion and what is actually happening to people. The pastor and prophet without the priest all too easily fall into promoting the organization and carping about the steady flow of bad news. What one cannot miss in places like San Fernando Cathedral and in the presence of people like Archbishop Tutu and the pentecostals of Latin America is the power and joy that come from preaching the gospel and celebrating the Eucharist in situations where the human condition is unavoidable but is transformed in the mystery of the incarnate Word. What would happen in a congregation that began to face the real human problems around it, the growing epidemic of AIDS, for example? How would that modify preaching? Would the congregation be content with infrequent celebration of the Eucharist? Would not pastoral and priestly functions merge with the task of preaching? Father Elizondo, for example, meets early on Tuesday mornings with the other pastoral ministers, to read the lections for the week. Together they reach some consensus about what needs to be preached; study and pastoral rounds add to that as the week unfolds. Once more, preaching is merged into the pastoral and priestly roles. Where the church engages the world, embodies the saving Word, *koinonia, diaconia*, and kerygma combine. That is exactly what one sees in a poor parish in San Antonio.

LITURGICAL PREACHING

In the most practical terms, what does liturgical preaching mean? What steps might we take toward this integration, toward preaching that participates fully in the work of the people of God? How might these images reshape our models of preaching and open new avenues toward more intentionally sacramental communities?

Preaching in Liturgy

A first step would be to get beyond the usual way of describing this relationship, that is, as preaching *and* liturgy. The present arrangement of theological studies in many of our seminaries and the professional alignments of those who teach perpetuate the idea that preaching can be done apart from a community's liturgical life. What is the relationship—we might ask those who form curriculum for our seminaries—between *lex credendi* and *lex orandi?*[14] If this question were dealt with seriously, homiletics might profitably move closer to liturgical studies, even toward becoming one discipline in that more comprehensive field. In any case, liturgical studies that included the preaching office would be given a larger place in the theological curriculum.

The reintegration of preaching into a more fully rounded worship might be advanced by relatively simple means. Even where there is no Communion, the order of service can be eucharistic, with the offering and prayers appearing at the same places as on communion Sunday. Simply by standing at the table for the prayers of the people and the Lord's Prayer, the presiding minister can gather the community in such a way as to connect the whole service with the Eucharist. (To effect this visual symbol, it would be important to keep the communion table clear, so that its proper use is always in view.) This will be all the more effective if the pastoral prayer—one more clericalism—gives way to bidding prayers that invite the congregation to do its liturgical work around the table, in a kind of "dry Communion." There is, of course, no substitute for breaking bread together.

The Lectionary

Preaching on the texts from the ecumenical lectionary connects preaching with liturgy. The preacher, from the beginning of preparation, recognizes the community's texts as the given, a place to begin and a gift of the tradition. The preacher does not spend time trying to "find a text," but in listening to what is placed before her or him. Where the lectionary becomes a tool of pastoral work, the texts find their way into nursing homes and study groups, board meetings and the pastor's teaching. Then many links are forged between the task of preaching and liturgical movement from Sunday to Sunday and season to season.

Some of our usual practices may be called into question as we seek to place preaching more fully in the liturgy. Topical preaching, titles for sermons, catchy series, even aiming at thematic unity in a given service—all of these might work against the integration we seek. The use of titles can connote that the sermon is solely the preacher's domain and can even decline to the level of advertising. Liturgy built around a theme, especially when the theme comes from the preacher working alone and without regard to the Christian year, may be unduly oriented toward the sermon. The thematic service can hold the congregation's nose too close to what the leader wants them to experience. The monolithic service often blunts the power of the liturgy's diversity and its appeal to the imagination and can serve to reinforce the idea against which we want to work, that the whole affair is a context for the preacher's performance.

The proliferation of translations of Scripture is, for all its boons to the student of Scripture, problematic for the liturgy. Many of us grew up with one version of Scripture, probably the Revised Standard Version or even the King James Version. We read and heard it at home, memorized it in Sunday school, and heard it from the pulpit. When the preacher wove the Scriptures into the sermon, the words were ours, and part of the power of preaching was the familiarity of ownership that the congregation felt. Would it not be an advantage liturgically if a congregation could agree on a common version for church school, family prayers, and worship? Preaching might be strengthened by a sense that, as someone put it, we were all singing out of the same hymnbook. Also, we would probably be better served, as preachers, to do away with the printed leaflets that orient the congregation not to participatory listening but to a more detached reading of printed material.

In addition to following the lectionary, there may also be some quite simple means of giving the congregation a new awareness of its ownership of preaching and a new sense that the sermon is—no less than prayer and offertory—a function of the community. Some communions provide the versicles that suggest this: The preacher and congregation stand together at the beginning of the sermon, to acknowledge the Trinity or to pray for the presence of the Holy

Spirit. However this is done—and it ought to be intentional—it suggests that what is about to happen is part of the work of the people. Just standing in the pulpit can be a way of acknowledging the community's ownership. I have several times been escorted to a high pulpit by a verger who then shut the gate after me! It is not unusual for congregations to assume that they own the preacher; how much better to cultivate a sense of owning preaching. The pulpit itself can be a powerful visual symbol of the ongoing life of the community, and the decision to forsake it for another spot should be carefully considered. As I have said elsewhere, the first consideration should not be communication per se, but the sense of communion.

Obviously much depends upon the pastor's self-understanding and even upon his or her deployment of time and resources. Does leading the congregation in worship mean that we must necessarily devote most of our time to preparing to preach? Can we do the work of preaching without its becoming a usurping, anxiety-producing preoccupation? How could the leader of worship move, in preparation and in the act of leading, toward being a worshiper? Is it possible to worship while we work?

Less Is More

Do we not need to make less of preaching in order to make it better? "Better" would mean well integrated into the community's worship, organic to the whole liturgical life of the congregation, not so burdensome or preoccupying as to produce undue anxiety, and evangelical in that we keep close to the essential gospel. Making less of preaching would mean putting it in its proper place, balancing the time and energy we give to the sermon with the contemplative time and careful planning required to preside well and confidently at liturgy.

A place to start toward this is in laying out the week's work. Monday read the texts as part of morning prayer or a time of quiet meditation, letting their images and language begin to arrange one's imaginative and spiritual life for the week. Live with the texts, take them on pastoral rounds and into the work of administration and teaching, jotting pad at hand. Toward the middle of the week read what the scholars have to say and pay attention to the collect and the psalm for the week, the hymnody and prayers appropriate for this particular Sunday. The week would include, of course, time for the arts, for being with a variety of people, for reading as widely as possible, and for a day-to-day liturgical life. By Thursday be writing the sermon and working through the liturgy. By Friday supper have all this arranged, including agreements with those who will assist in leading Sunday's service. Have you assured that there are people looking after all those other important details, from music and readers, bread and wine, linen and flowers, to greeters and the social hour, all important to the comprehensive event of Sunday morning?

Then take much of Saturday off, doing the things that let mind and body go free. Use this day, too, for finishing preparation. Do that by finding some quiet and relaxed time to vocalize the entire service, reading through the propers and prayers and talking through the sermon in a way that allows in advance for enjoying the work you have done and assuring yourself of the clarity and integration of the event to come.

Another way of putting it is this: To make less of preaching in order to make it more, we must live life as deeply as we can and then make something of that in the gathered community. On Sunday we bring our joys and sorrows into holy time and space, to prayer. We bring our offerings, the fruit of our own bodies and blood poured out in work, and mix them with the bread and wine that Jesus shares with sinners in Eucharist. And right there, where we pray and make Eucharist, we bring our words, the images and stories of our life together, and connect that with the Scripture. That is preaching, and it is both less and more than it has been for many of us.

Tuning the Sermon

For an example of liturgical preaching, consider the homiletics of Holy Week. It is possible to "tune" the sermon to the liturgy by attention to the movement of the week and to the mood, tone, and language of each occasion. Each day, from Palm Sunday to the Triduum, has its particular characteristics, grounded in the christological drama and in both catholic and local tradition. As an example of preaching that takes its cues from liturgy, rather than the other way around, let us briefly consider some of the possibilities for preaching during Holy Week.

Palm Sunday, or Passion Sunday, offers a particular opportunity to the preacher. If the homily, like the Gospel of the entry into Jerusalem, is given in the course of the procession, the preacher actually participates in the movement of the liturgy, and the sermon becomes one step on the way to the cross. Putting the sermon in such a position—the processional hymn simply stops when the preacher is in the midst of the congregation and resumes after the homily ends—subordinates the preacher to the later reading of the passion narrative, on which it is hardly possible to preach anyway. In the procession, preaching, as it were, on the way, the preacher participates in the first part of Holy Week's journey and joins in the ironic mood of the day: We are not able to say unambiguously what we mean by the kingship of Jesus. So we will, preacher and congregation, wave our palms and follow Jesus toward the place where his true royalty will be revealed. This is a day of drama, of music and hosannas, and of a well-worn story, in which the preacher participates by the placement of the homily in the midst of the liturgical action.

The evening service on Maundy Thursday is a family occasion, and preaching at this service is table talk. The sermon will almost certainly echo the language peculiar to this event, such as that found in John's account of the footwashing: "Love one another, as I have loved you." We would be surprised if the homily did not recall this language, just as we would not be well served if the preacher's mood did not reflect the affirmation and celebration of the pivotal ritual of the church, Holy Communion. The texts for preaching on this evening, both the Epistle and the Gospel, contain the words at the center of the Eucharist, the words of institution, so that the preacher on this night stands on especially holy ground. That the homily is brief and modest does not mean that it is to be taken lightly or done in an off-hand way. Rather, the preacher is in a position not unlike trying to find the right words for a funeral or a wedding: Less is more, and the economy of words points only to the weight of the event. Here we, God's people, gather around the holy table, remembering Jesus and giving thanks for that first supper and for all that have followed from it. The occasion tells the preacher what and how to preach.

At the Good Friday service, usually from noon until three, the preacher may well be given the texts directly from the collage of the Gospel accounts of Jesus' sayings on the cross, the "seven words." Here is an obvious example of liturgy determining the content and, in fact, the length and mood of the homily. Anyone who has preached on the seven words over those three hours will have been amazed at how quickly the times goes by, and will understand what is being described here: that the liturgy takes over the preacher, carrying him or her along, setting limits on what can be said, making up in its music and drama, its silence and starkness, for the preacher's inability on such an occasion.

One movement of the liturgy, seen more and more on Good Friday, is the procession to the cross. A large wooden cross is carried into the church, down the center aisle, by a person who, stopping at intervals, calls out: "The cross of Christ." This cross is then placed at the front of the church for all to look upon. The preacher would do well to echo these words in the homily, perhaps in fact to make them the last words of the homily, and so tie the homily into the drama of the day. Wherever the preacher can echo the liturgy, the sermon will be strengthened by its connection with the people's work. The preacher's task on these occasions is not to be novel, but to enter into what is happening. An important part of the preparation to preach on this day is going over the rite for the day, reading through the prayers, the rubrics, and the hymns that are usually sung on this occasion. What do the people do on this day, and how can the preacher mirror, echo, and complement their work? Someone has said that the American Thanksgiving is a wonderful holiday because it is so unambiguous: Everyone knows exactly what to do, so that all one has to do is cook the turkey well, be sure there is cranberry sauce and stuffing, and keep to the ritual of the day! Preachers could learn from that the benefits of entering into a ritual that has its own shape, color, and movement.

The Great Vigil of Easter, kept in an increasing number of churches, has at its center the powerful image of light, by contrast to the tomb's darkness on Holy Saturday. A new fire is kindled at the entrance to the church, from which the paschal candle is lighted. As the candle, to burn throughout the fifty days of Easter, is carried into the church, the bearer of the light and the congregation join in

the response, "The light of Christ! The light of Christ!" Then the
cantor leads in the Exsultet, with its repeated litany: "This is the
night.... This is the night...." The drama of the light and this rep-
etitious language give the preacher the lyrical idiom of the homily,
and the sermon can hardly help echoing "The light of Christ" and
"This is the night when Christ broke the bonds...." (One can easily imagine a black preacher ringing the changes on this liturgical
language.) As if this were not enough, this is also the night of Baptism; following ancient custom, those who have been preparing in
Lent are now received into the church. The preacher might give
the homily at the baptistry on this occasion, as one way of connecting with this powerful drama of life out of death, of entering into
the darkness and emerging into the light of Christ.[15]

Obviously the sermon on Easter aims to evoke the acclamation of
that day, so that to the preacher's "Christ is risen!" the congregation
responds, "The Lord is risen indeed!" Everyone present is there to
hear this call and to make this response, in music and prayer, in the
Eucharist, and at the pulpit. The preacher who uses this occasion
to try to argue for the resurrection makes a big mistake, acting
as if this event depended upon prowess in the pulpit. This is an
occasion that belongs to the faithful, and the preacher does well to
be carried along by the event and to sing, in the sermon, one more
alleluia! This does not mean that the preacher might not introduce a
contrapuntal realism, or even a note of discord, but the sermon must
finally join in the common acclamation, "Christ is risen!" Anyone
who has preached at Easter will know the truth of this. Here, of
all days of the year, preaching is put in its proper place and the
preacher is called to be no more and no less than the voice of Christ's
body.

An Analogy

To put what I have been saying in another way: It is what the
people bring to worship that gives preaching its shape and content.
Donald Coggan, former archbishop of Canterbury and splendid
evangelical preacher, describes the close analogy between bread
and wine, in the Eucharist, and local idiom in the sermon:

> In [the] central service of the Church certain elements, the elements
> of bread and wine, given to us by God, are presented by the people.

"Through your goodness we have this bread to offer which earth has given and human hands have made." We pray that "by the power of your Holy Spirit these gifts of bread and wine may be to us his body and his blood," and that "as we eat and drink these holy gifts" God will "renew us by your Spirit, inspire us with your love, and unite us in the body of your Son."

So it is in preaching. The "elements" are words, ordinary words, the words that we constantly use in the commerce of everyday life. But in preaching, the life-giving Spirit takes these words and makes them vehicles of his grace. He fashions words into the Word. Who can doubt that, when such preaching takes place, there is the Real Presence of Christ?[16]

In such an analogy, preaching emerges as an act of the whole community, in which one person—pastor, prophet, and priest— offers to God the life of these particular people at this time and place. The images and stories, the vernacular and the style, are to a large degree gifts of the people as much as the bread and wine, which among the earliest Christians were brought from kitchen to altar. The preacher embodies the Word, not just as a man or woman with the Word from on high, but as a person in community with words that come in off the street and move toward renewed thanksgiving and grateful service.

The large doors of St. Peter's Church, my parish, open onto the main street of Morristown, New Jersey. In good weather the sexton leaves them open on Sunday morning, giving anyone at the pulpit or altar a clear view of the life of our town passing by. Preacher and priest look down the wide aisle, beyond the congregation, to the world outside, the noise of its occasional emergencies sometimes drowning out our preaching and prayers. Given the analogy between Word and Sacrament, that is as it should be: Both come in off the street of our common life to be the vehicles of holy Word and Holy Communion.

This is a two-way street: the gifts of the people, the gifts of God, for the people of God. As close as I have come to this was in the small Xhosa villages near the Federal Theological Seminary where I once taught, in South Africa, at the continent's southernmost tip. One of my duties on Sundays was to drop students at their charges and, more often than not, to preside at Holy Communion in one of these remote churches. There were no church buildings; we usually used someone's dining table pulled out into the hard-earth courtyard among the thatch-roofed rondavels that formed a family's compound. From somewhere would come a linen cloth and an eager circle of women, men, and children. We took bread with us, large crusty loaves, one of which was placed on the table with local wine. The sermon was given near the table; prayers were said with all standing around; then we had Communion.

Afterward, my student, the elders of the village, and I would walk from house to house, giving the bread and cup to those unable to come to the service. The other thing was that we took those extra loaves of bread with us, Sunday's midday meal for some who would have little else. It was almost in the same breath that we would say: "the body of Christ" and "here is your lunch." Isn't that what we hope for, as preachers and members of the church, that in our work and worship, as daily food and holy bread mingle, prophetic Word and Holy Sacrament might be one?

4
A Down-to-earth Rhetoric

So the Word became flesh and dwelt among us, full of grace and truth.
—John 1:14

Our faith imposes on us a right and duty to throw ourselves into the things of the earth.
—Teilhard de Chardin, *The Divine Milieu*

For Christians, the mystery of the Incarnation consists in the revelation that God became totally enfleshed, as thoroughly animalized as ourselves.
—Matthew Fox, *Original Blessing*

Does it follow from the cardinal doctrine of the Christian faith—that the divine has taken the form of a particular human being—that there is a rhetoric particularly suited to such an affirmation? Is there a style appropriate to the gospel, and if so, what would that be? This chapter will attempt to make a case for such a rhetoric of Christian proclamation and to describe its essential characteristics.

This is not a new question. The particular characteristics of the Gospels themselves betray a certain rhetorical self-consciousness from the earliest days of the church. It is as if the early Christians kept asking themselves: How shall we put this? And today there is keen attention to style among preachers, both those who are trying to lead a local congregation and television personalities whose enterprise depends upon commanding a vast audience. The story of Jesus and the biblical tradition surrounding that have probably never been presented in such diverse and self-conscious styles as one can find any Sunday on the various media and in the churches, from slick Hollywood hype to old-fashioned revival hour, from an accommodating sophistication to belligerent crusade. But could we not say that, in general, today's styles come not so much from reflection on the nature of the gospel and a rhetoric appropriate to that, but rather from a pragmatic consideration: What will get and hold an audience?

Infinitely prior to that concern, however, is the first question raised in this chapter, a question that rises from the fundamental confession of each Christian that God has appeared among us in the man Jesus of Nazareth. How we witness to that, no less than what we believe and proclaim, should issue from faith's confession. The grounds for a rhetoric appropriate to the church lie in the very appearance of Jesus, as a human being who walked the earth, as well as in his own speech about God.

A RHETORIC OF FAITH

Some years ago an accrediting team visited the seminary in which I teach. One of the visitors asked about the content of the basic course in homiletics, and, among other things, the videotaping of students' sermons came up. "As I understand it, at the end of the course the student passes the videotape test," the evaluator said, in a way that seemed not to value attention to method. The evaluator's concern was with the more abstract and theoretical aspects of theological education, and the emphasis in homiletical instruction on matters of style and delivery was called into question. But in the work of preaching it is not possible to separate form from content, style from substance. Even the tone in which a sermon is spoken can be theologically revealing. Take for example the word *God*, the many ways in which it can be pronounced, enunciated, stressed. Much of a preacher's theology can be read from the manner in which this word is used, not only the tone in which it is spoken but the frequency and context of its appearance in the sermon. The material the preacher chooses, the way in which it is arranged, and the style in which it is spoken: All are comprised by what we might call a rhetoric of faith.

Fred Craddock has paid close attention to this. He writes, in the context of emphasizing homiletical method:

Vague as it may seem at first, there is such a thing as appropriate style, a style that fits, a style that is part of the very fabric of an occasion, of a relationship, of an event, of the truth. We recognize it when it is present, and we are so aware of its absence that we may have no choice but to stomp out of the room to escape the insult, even if that room be a sanctuary. There is such a thing as a *Christian* style, a method of communicating congenial to the nature of the Christian faith.[1]

"There is such a thing as . . . a method of communicating congenial to the Christian faith": That is the thesis of this chapter, a thesis that opens us more toward the ancient liturgies of the church, toward the earth and its many creatures and cultures, and toward the arts that come from the brain, ear, eye, and hand of humanity. We can make this assertion because of the gospel itself, the story of the creating Word become flesh, walking and loving the earth, and also because of the style in which Jesus himself preached.

Storytelling and the Gospel

Amos Wilder has done a great deal toward describing a rhetoric of faith. In his pioneering book *Early Christian Rhetoric,* Wilder shows how the very nature of the gospel led the primitive church to express itself in certain ways, especially in the form of the story:

> One of the earliest and most important rhetorical forms in the Church was the story. This is theologically significant. The new movement of the Gospel was not to be identified with a new teaching or a new experience but with an action and therefore a history. The revelation was in an historical drama. The narrative mode inevitably imposed itself as the believers rehearsed this saving action, including particular scenes of it that played themselves out in the market-place or the Temple-court, at a dinner with guests or in a synagogue. The locus of the new faith was in concrete human relationships and encounters. Therefore the new community, living out a new kind of human and divine relationship, naturally rehearsed models of Jesus' actions and interactions, since it was through these that the saving work of God had initiated its course. With this kind of God the story was the proper kind of witness.[2]

The church, in trying to give expression to what had dawned upon it in Jesus, looked for the most plastic forms of expression, the most open and malleable images and language available. The narrative form, story, was the most suitable, the indispensable medium of this gospel.

This is owing, in part, to the fact that among all cultures storytelling is the most common means of expressing and symbolizing faith. But, as Wilder shows, the Christian faith has a particular need for the story. Jesus, as teacher and preacher (Can we really distinguish those roles in his ministry?), clearly had an affinity for the story. The primary form of Jesus' wisdom and his eschatological proclamation is the parable. On occasion, it seems that he used more specifically theological language to alert his hearers to the reign of God at hand: For example, in the Gospels he speaks of the judgment, the figure of the Messiah, the life of the age to come, and the heavenly Son of man. But for the most part he is reticent even in using the name of God, and relies largely on what we would call "lay" language. In the most commonplace similes and stories, Jesus sets forth his understanding of God and, as Wilder would say, his own faith.

> That storytelling had such a central place in the very beginning of the Gospel means more than may at first appear. It is not enough to say that Jesus used the form of the parable only as a good pedagogical strategy. It was not merely to hold the attention of his hearers that he told stories or took good illustrations out of his file. There was something in the nature of the case that evoked this rhetoric, something in the nature of the Gospel. At the very least there is the assumption that action is significant, and that the varied activities, pursuits, and vocations of men's life in nature are fateful.[3]

It is generally agreed that of all texts in the Bible, the parables lie closest to the original expressions of the historical Jesus. Wilder assumes this, and he is confident, as are more recent students of the parables such as John Dominic Crossan[4] and James Breech,[5] that we can discern from the parables Jesus' own preaching.

Parables and Theology

What are the characteristics of Jesus' preaching as we see it in the parables? Following Wilder's lead, we can sketch a rhetoric of Christian proclamation based on Jesus' own style of imaginative, parabolic speech, including not only the extended narratives but his various uses of analogy, simile, and even hyperbole.

Human-centered and Realistic Speech.   First of all, the parables are completely human and realistic. The imagination of Jesus is down-to-earth (Where else might imagination get its material?), and the power of his speech is not in explicit reference to theology, but in its earthiness. Wilder uses the word "secularity" to describe the parables and sees their authenticity as immediate and realistic. To be sure, we have here the language of revelation, but Jesus is not giving us moral examples or veiled piety: This is language that changes things by revealing a new reality.

But this revelation, in a way completely congruent with who Jesus is as the Christ, is in earthly garb. Jesus' speech embodies our confession: In this very human being, the Word of God has taken flesh. That could be the definition of a parable, of a sermon, as well as of what it means to be a confessing Christian. The presence among us of this man and, as a corollary to that, the presence among us of this speech, reveal the presence of God. Wilder quotes Gerhard Ebeling: "The art of the parable . . . is none other than that of bringing the hearer face to face with what it is to be human and thereby to make clear what it means for God to draw near."[6] Edmund Steimle, assuming that the Bible itself has this character—that in its actual content it is more secular than sacred, to use the conventional terminology—asserts that if we followed the Bible's lead our preaching like that of Jesus would be much more worldly, more steeped in the secular, than it now is. Steimle liked reminding his students at Union Theological Seminary that "the sermon which starts in the Bible and stays in the Bible is not biblical."[7]

Jesus' preaching moved outside the conventional speech of the religious establishment. How else are we to interpret Matthew's conclusion to the Sermon on the Mount: "And when Jesus had finished these sayings, the crowds were astonished at his teaching, for he taught them as one who had authority, and not as their scribes" (Matt. 7:28-29)? The most obvious characteristic of his teaching is its unpretentious confidence in ordinary things and common human experience to bear the revelation of God's presence.

However, when it comes to preaching, we are often uncomfortable with such earthy language. For example, at the seminary where I teach I heard a young preacher give an interpretation of Luke's parables of the lost sheep and the lost coin. At the seminary we were trying to get beyond sexually exclusive language, and in the midst of his interpretation the preacher stated: "God is both the shepherd and the woman, male and female." Although the point may be one to be made (misleading as it is in turning the metaphors toward actual correspondence to the being of God, who is neither male nor female), the nature of the parables does not support such an exegesis. In the story, the shepherd is a shepherd, the sheep a sheep, both smelling of manure. The images in the Hebrew Scriptures of Yahweh caring for Israel like a shepherd, the messianic images of the great and hoped-for shepherd, and the Gospels' metaphors of Christ as shepherd make it almost inevitable that we will assimilate these parables in Luke to those theological and christological associations. But to do so is to turn parable toward allegory and away from the earthy realism in which the power of Jesus' speech lies.

Paul Ricoeur, in an essay on the difficulty of our hearing the parables of Jesus, writes:

> The first thing that may strike us is that the Parables are radically profane stories. There are no gods, no demons, no angels, no miracles, no time before time, as in the creation stories, not even founding events as in the Exodus account. Nothing like that, but precisely people like us: Palestinian landlords traveling and renting their fields, stewards and workers, sowers and fishers, fathers and sons; in a word, ordinary people doing ordinary things: selling and buying, letting down a net into the sea and so on. Here resides the initial paradox: on the one hand these stories are—as a critic said—narratives of normalcy—but on the other hand, it is the Kingdom of God that is said to be like this. The paradox is that the *extraordinary* is *like* the *ordinary*.[8]

The images and stories of Jesus, aimed at helping us see things as they really are (that God is present to human life), stay close to things as they are. The style of the parables—down-to-earth material, simple structure, the storyteller's economy and willingness to trust the story—reveals a theological point of view: God is present to human life, "the reign of God is at hand." As Wilder puts it, "Jesus [in the way he speaks] shows that for him human destiny is at stake in ordinary creaturely existence—domestic, economic, social. This is the way God made us. The world is real. Time is real. Man is a toiler and an 'acter,' and a chooser."[9] In precise observation, reliance on the actual, and the refusal to substitute concepts for concrete stories and images, Jesus the teller of parables reveals his own faith; his rhetoric, his style, is at one with his faith and the theological assertions that spring from it, and that rhetoric is thus the basis for the appropriate means of preaching and teaching the gospel. The parables of Jesus answer, once and for all, a question that is perennial in homiletics: What is the place of human experience in the preaching of the gospel? The parables are grounded in human life: That is where the Word of God appears.

The Elegance of Prophetic Speech. A second characteristic of the parables is their elegance: Nothing is in excess, nothing is wasted, all is disciplined to the singular vision of the artist. The parables of Jesus reveal what it is to be "pure in heart," in speech that issues unwaveringly from Jesus' own experience of the presence of God to human life. Clear and simple in his speech, of the earth and earthy, Jesus reveals in the elegance of this style both his faith and his eschatological urgency. He does not give illustrations—the rabbis could do that—but he confronts his hearers with the direct speech of life at hand, speech in which the reign of God is revealed in its radical, undeniable immediacy. The parables are eschatological, and that is revealed in their elegance: They spring from a single act of total vision. Here is language inextricable from the present moment, from the observable situation in which human life stands, language that in its clarity and simplicity will not allow us to escape Jesus' prophetic keenness.

The parables are never discursive or argumentative: They are declarative in the way that a fine painting or true-to-life play is. The aim of the teller of parables, like that of the artist, is recognition, a sudden and undeniable seeing of things as they are. Dorothy Sayers links recognition and revelation:

> This recognition of truth which we get in the artist's work comes to us as a revelation of new truth. . . . I am not referring to the sort of patronising recognition we give to a writer by nodding our heads and observing: "Yes, yes, very good, very true—that's just what I've always been saying." I mean the recognition of a truth which tells us something about ourselves that we had *not* been "always saying"—something which puts a new knowledge of ourselves within our grasp. It is new, startling, and perhaps shattering—and yet it comes to us with a sense of familiarity.[10]

This could be a description of the art of the parable, or of preaching. Here is the language of the moment, given to the simplicity of expression that springs from the artist's attention to what is actually at hand and his or her seeing in that what is of ultimate consequence. What word better describes Van Gogh's paintings—of a pair of old shoes, a hospital bed, a vase of irises—than *elegant?* Are not the parables of Jesus in the same style, equally restrained, limited by their attachment to the commonplace? Can we doubt that the elegance that we see in both the parables and the paintings rises from and aims toward what Sayers calls *recognition*, a sudden seeing that is ultimately transforming?

One consequence of this mode of expression is that it cuts us off from argumentation. It is as impossible to argue with a parable as with a painting. One might be disturbed by it, disoriented and even angered, but argument is out of the question. Choose any parable and try to argue with it. One cannot because the parable is simply what it is: a picture of agricultural life, of what happens in a family or with a seed. Someone has described the parable as "a nice little story which when you are not looking knocks you flat"; and Eduard Riegert defines parable as "a verbal hand-grenade."[11] The only possible responses are giving way to the shattering, world-dismantling power of the parable, or rejection of the teller of the parable, discounting both the teller and the teller's speech. It is for this reason that some have said that Jesus was crucified for telling the parables.[12]

To those whose whole way of seeing the world is threatened by the integrity of those who tell parables and their art, the parable can be maddening in its elegant, undeniable simplicity. What am I to do with a new way of seeing the world—revealed in the idiom of the very world in which I live—and a person whose every word and action reveals the presence of the holy? It is what we might call the elegance of this style that makes that question unavoidable. W. B. Yeats—who believed that the only irresistible poetry is that which does not cry out, teach, condescend, or explain—wrote: "Indeed, only those things which seem useless or very feeble have any power."[13] The elegance of Jesus' style is like the beauty of his person: Both are grounded in ironic earthiness and simplicity. As with good poetry, there is more here than immediately meets the eye.

The Spoken Word. A third characteristic of the style of the parables is that they were originally spoken, and most likely in situations
of conflict. The word *elegance* should not lead us to the idea of parable as literary, in the sense of a refined prose piece. There is no
reason to take the simple form and clarity of the parable as signs of
literary polishing. Rather, we can imagine that they originated in
prophetic innovation, coming as gifted words to meet the demands
of the moment. Amos Wilder calls the parables "scenarios of life and
destiny" that present alternative possibilities for human thought
and action.[14] They have about them the freshness of speech, and
those today who take the parables as material and model for preaching can be guided by this oral quality of Jesus' storytelling and
image-making.

   We may be sure that the parables were spoken in an ironic—not a
heroic—style, and we can probably assume that the storyteller was
given to the comic mode, the style of one who doodles in the dirt as
he faces questions of life and death, waiting for the needed language
to present itself (see John 7:53—8:11). The rhetoric of faith is in the
style of speech, appropriate to the Word which is constantly taking
flesh, meeting us in daily life, dwelling among us. As H. H. Farmer
has shown, speech—as opposed to writing—is the medium of the
Christian faith. The unmediated vibrations moving from larynx to
eardrum, accompanied by facial expression and bodily movement,
can express the gospel, the mingling of "ultimate demand and final
succour," like no other medium.[15] The parables of Jesus, as speech,
make a direct claim on their hearers, but not in the form of argument
or in the complexities of written discourse. They have the direct,
unavoidable appeal of a person speaking in an ironic, perhaps even
comic mode.

   This preaching of Jesus, if we took it as a homiletical model,
imposes a clear critique on contemporary homiletics. Many sermons are not in the language of speech at all, but attempt a literary
style. The highly illustrated, sometimes overblown sermon betrays
quite a different understanding of the efficacy of human speech
than is presupposed by the parables. In Jesus' preaching, less is
more, and excess would actually diminish the power of this economical speech. To get his message across, Jesus deliberately chose
to say less, not more; as we have seen, this decision derives from

the nature of the gospel itself. This gospel is suitably reticent and understated, leaving room for faith's apprehension and decision. A poem by Emily Dickinson suggests the difference between the style of Jesus and the rhetoric of overconfidence and certitude:

> He preached upon "breadth" till it argued him narrow,—
> The broad are too broad to define;
> And of "truth" until it proclaimed him a liar,—
> The truth never flaunted a sign.
>
> Simplicity fled from his counterfeit presence
> As gold the pyrites would shun.
> What confusion would cover the innocent Jesus
> To meet so enabled a man![16]

It is just this modesty of speech that points to the immense mystery that Jesus apprehends and that comes to ironic expression in his earthy stories, his life, and his death. And that is what is at stake theologically for the preacher who monitors her or his speech by Jesus' ironic preaching.

EIRON AS ICON

Comic irony—which responds to our sense of the distance between what is and what ought to be and exposes pretense and wrongheadedness—employs the figure of the *eiron*, the understated person who appears to be less than he or she is.[17] The hero, on the other hand, is the larger-than-life figure who is trumped up to be more than the human condition will bear: the champion, the invincible warrior, or the pompous fool. As Morris Niedenthal sees it, a good example of the hero is Donald Duck, thoroughly impressed with himself and completely self-confident.[18] The *eiron*, by contrast, is given to understatement and is a more considerable person than meets the eye.

Metaphor's Low Door

Charlie Chaplin, for example, personifies the ironic. Picture this game little man in the film *Modern Times*. He is working on an assembly line, with the boss in a glass booth above, controlling the speed of the moving belt. Charlie's job is to tighten two nuts as they go by, faster and faster. Technology seems to get the best of him, even to humiliate him with the "feeding machine" designed to let him work while he eats corn-on-the-cob and cream pie. But in his persistence, in his unwillingness to take himself too seriously, and in the quality of his vision (he daydreams of a house in the country, life close to nature, simple pleasures), his humanity shines through. This is the ironic person, a mode of being human that is congenial to the Christian faith.

There is at the very center of the Christian religion both a person and a literature distinctly in the ironic mode. The controversial movie based on Kazantzakis's novel *The Last Temptation of Christ*[19] is problematic for different persons for different reasons, but one point at which it offends our heroic culture and perhaps a church too much tempted by heroism is its portrait of Jesus not easily recognizable as the Christ. This, of course, is nothing new: From the time of the Gospels' composition until now we have confronted the figure who, as Schweitzer said, comes to us as one unknown. The ironic mode of Jesus' life and teaching has, however, been obscured from the very beginning by the church's accumulating devotion to the Christ whom we have seen in Jesus.

But access to the way of Jesus is, as John Dominic Crossan says, "by the low door of metaphor." In Jesus' life and work emerges a radically new vision of what it is to be human before God; this vision is "so alien to consciousness that this referent can be grasped only within the metaphor itself."[20] This means that the world, in its concrete particularity, as Jesus presents it in his lowly stories of shepherds, housewives, parents, and children, is "the house of God." Jesus' telling of the parables stems from his seeking to express what is permanently inexpressible. "Here it is not a question of imagining at the limits of one's imagination but rather of imagining whole new ways of imagining."[21]

James Breech, like Crossan, believes that Jesus was constantly in the prophetic situation, confronted by people who were not just recalcitrant but unable to receive the proclamation of God's merciful presence and the openness of the reign of God to all. Indeed, says Breech, the idea of the kingdom had become so self-serving and wedded to heroic notions of the nation that Jesus kept silent on these expectations. In his parables Jesus is confronting the entrenched resentment of his hearers against himself as a free person and against those set free by the gospel. The parables rise from Jesus' own freedom from the categories of sin, guilt, and death, and they call on his hearers to embrace God present as mercy in every circumstance of life. Breech's thesis emerges in a series of questions provoked by the parables. He quotes T. S. Eliot's "Burnt Norton": "Human kind / Cannot bear very much reality."[22] Breech goes on to ask:

> Is it possible to conceive of a mode of being human that is not an expression of discontent with the actual but could affirm the concrete world and real human beings in their otherness without taking refuge in other-worldliness, self-hatred, or inwardness? Is discriminating awareness of particular individuals compatible with unsentimental love? What then would love be—a passion for the actual?[23]

For an excellent example of this "passion for the actual," in the form of a contemporary parable, see Fred Craddock's story of an old man and his dog, in *Overhearing the Gospel*.[24]

Breech makes a great deal of the definition of parables that we learned in Sunday school: "A parable is an earthly story with a heavenly meaning." Jesus' parables—nice little stories that, when we are not looking, knock us flat—force us to look at this world, to take seriously the phenomena of human actions, to look directly at human beings, even to delight in all mortal things, in the shade of red in the blanket on a bed in Van Gogh's room at Arles, in "the dachshund shimmying with ecstasy."[25]

The Good Samaritan

Let us take as an example of this earthy, ironic rhetoric a narrative that has evolved from parable to example story to iconic language, Luke 10:25-37. In its earliest redaction this story was turned into an example of neighborliness, and we have in most of our teaching and preaching received it as such. But the central character would certainly not have been a heroic example to be imitated: That would have done us little good anyway because, as someone said, nothing is so burdensome as a good example. Here is the *eiron* of *eirons*: the despised outsider, unfit as a companion at table or at worship, the ostracized half-breed. He appears to be, on the surface, so much less than he turns out to be, his capacity to be human beyond the imaginative reach of Jesus' auditors. The parable depends for its power on this biased perception of the Samaritan, and on the understated development of the story. All the conventional auditors can see is a stereotype; all the Samaritan sees is the wounded man, this very person in need. The story unfolds with sixty-six words devoted to the Samaritan's action—active verbs and concrete nouns—so that the hearer cannot evade or rationalize the Samaritan's goodness or ignore his radical freedom from resentment and hatred. Long before the parable was a call to dutiful neighborliness, it was a picture of an inexplicably free man, a story that in its appeal to the imagination could set the will free. The result is a whole new vista in which the receiver of the parable is freed to follow Jesus into a new future. The ironic parable, in fact, comes to function as an icon. That is, rather than a hero story to be imitated, it is a human, if artistic, picture that opens us toward God's realm. We are called to contemplate, and it is this contemplation that leads to transformation. We actually experience, in this recognizable human story, the presence of God: *Eiron*, in parabolic form, becomes icon.

Remarkably, the parable, familiar as it is, may still function as icon for us. Although we cannot experience the story as its first hearers did (they easily identified and just as easily despised the Samaritan), it is raised by constant use in liturgy to the level of icon. We might name other narratives from Scripture, including the twenty-third psalm and the parable of the prodigal, but it is certain that the parable of the Samaritan functions in this way. Its authentic, undeniable humanity and its earthy concreteness appeal to our imagination, and in contemplation of this merciful figure, so undeniably human, we behold the Christ.

Faith's Poetic

The church, at its best, lives by its imagination. W. H. Auden once remarked that it is difficult to be a Christian if one is not a poet. Whether we are interpreting Scripture, listening to a sermon, singing hymns, celebrating the Eucharist, or trying to weep with those who weep and rejoice with those who rejoice, without a lively imagination we do not fully succeed.[26]

Take the Scriptures, for example. What happens when the literal mind takes over and all is hardened into fact, moral code, and program? The disputatious and legalistic preoccupations of a good part of American Christianity can be attributed in no small part to a failure of the imagination. Much of the power of Scripture is the power of story, metaphor, poetry, the compelling narrative, and the colorful personality. Without imagination it becomes just so many wooden texts to be used for buttressing one position or another, as when Jesus' liberating story of the Samaritan is reduced to admonition. What is more, the Bible loses, when imagination declines, the power of particularity, and it all becomes *The Bible*, all of equal weight, monochrome, wanting in human vitality.

Edmund Steimle had this in mind when he urged the preacher to be more biblical by being more secular, in touch with earth and things earthy. Just as the Bible ranges over the terrain of the human situation, so the sermon that takes its cue from Scripture will be worldly, saturated with life. One of the real challenges facing the preacher is to bring imagination to the biblical literature, to get past the "sermon text" to really see and hear the people in the narratives, to enter these stories with the eyes of one hoping to see, as in an icon or a human face, the face of Christ.[27]

The poetic mind is indispensable to the Christian life. Without the capacity to allow one thing to stand for another, to see more than is there, we could not get far with keeping the Christian year (Is November 1 just another day in late fall or All Saints?), hearing the Word of God from another human being, or finding the presence of God in ordinary bread and wine. If God in Christ is present to us under these species, in our common life, then faith's profile is not far from imagination, which can enter in, receive as a child, and apprehend the holy in the mundane actuality of this world, and especially in the contradictions of our lives. Paul Scott Wilson has offered an excellent treatment of the working of the imagination and its dependence on everyday experience.[28] Imagination, he says, is sparked by juxtaposition, especially of the earthy and what we normally identify as the sacred. Or consider Flannery O'Connor and her powerful sense of the sacramental presence of God in the material world. One could speak also of the theology of Matthew Fox and his esteem for Native Americans, who managed through thousands of years of profound spirituality to bring together earth and spirit.[29] This is the way of imaginative spirituality and, for us, of sacramental Christianity in which bread of earth and bread of heaven combine, and where under the unmistakable signs of our humanity, seen clearly in the suffering and death of Jesus, we are delivered from sin and death into a life of grateful service.

The Christ Figure

All Christ figures are necessarily imperfect, and in their imperfection they point toward the Christ. All metaphors function in that manner: They point by their dissimilarity as well as by their likeness. Jesus becomes, for us, the supreme *eiron*, who in human form reveals, to those who by faith can see, the eternal God. As *eiron*, he demands our close attention, and when he speaks, particularly in the parables, he demands we lend a careful ear. As icon, the ironic Christ directs our gaze beyond himself, and every attempt to represent this Christ must also retire before the mystery, the *eiron* become icon. So we spread our all too human board, and speak of what he was and did, and the divine comes close. We stand up to preach and hope that every sermon, also *eiron* and icon, will lead us toward the table where the true host welcomes us.

James Breech is convinced that the setting of the Lord's Prayer is the eucharistic table, where we acknowledge what it is to be human—hungry, tempted, in constant need of forgiveness and of the courage to forgive; thus we pray in confidence, "Our Father ...thy kingdom come...," at the very place where we are being fed.[30] In his sermon on the second petition of the Lord's Prayer, Gerhard Ebeling connects that petition with preaching:

> For to pray in the name of Jesus for the coming of God's kingdom is to pray not for the absent but for the present kingdom of God, not a kingdom whose time is not yet come, but for the kingdom whose time was long ago proclaimed in every sermon and every testimony to Jesus Christ: "Behold, now is the acceptable time; behold now is the day of salvation" (II Cor. 6:2). This is a kingdom for whose coming we can pray calmly and confidently because it is one that has already come and is constantly coming.[31]

To see this requires no less imagination than faith. Without imagination we are incapable of grasping the presence of God in the down-to-earth story of Jesus, and we will fail to understand fully what those who knew Jesus witness to us, that in this ironic figure the creative Word was manifest.

THE CONCISE HOMILY

An obvious starting point, if we are to move our preaching closer to the model that we find in Jesus, is an effort at economy of speech. The concise homily, though still rare in Protestant churches, is the emerging homiletical form. This is not to say that it is new: Roman Catholics and, to a lesser degree, Anglicans are accustomed to brief homilies at the Eucharist. This is in part a matter of necessity: If the Communion is to be celebrated properly there usually is not time for an extended sermon. Also, reducing the time given to the sermon is a powerful symbol in the more Catholic traditions of the primacy of the Eucharist. Reticence, too, is itself a testimony to mystery and holiness; no matter how long we talk, we can never put the mystery into words. At the same time, the Word of God indeed appears in our modest speech. The brief homily, sometimes little more than a comment on the connection of one or more of the texts to the liturgical occasion, is, we might say, "liturgy-friendly" and by its very reticence appropriate to declaring the mystery of faith.

But perhaps most Protestants would consider the brief homily as something other than preaching. When, in these churches, on communion Sunday the sermon is pared down it is often referred to as a "meditation." Many Protestant churchgoers in North America would consider themselves somehow cheated if the preacher stopped short of fifteen minutes, and some congregations would expect a sermon of twice that length. No doubt many clergy would have the nagging feeling of not earning their pay if the sermon stopped at eight minutes. In the black tradition, the preacher has not even warmed up in ten minutes, and it is certainly true that each of us needs a different amount of time in order to accomplish what we set out to achieve in our sermons. Moving toward more economical preaching would face considerable objection, and proponents of this move need to be sensitive to the established practice and deep feelings of different communions.

One argument for shorter sermons is, of course, the reduced attention-span of people who are conditioned by the electronic media. The public speaker, even the preacher, may have difficulty holding an audience beyond fifteen minutes; the longest space between commercials on television is about fourteen minutes. Many preachers have adjusted the length of their sermons to this fact.

Theological and Liturgical Considerations

More important than the limits of the congregation's attention-span are the theological and liturgical reasons for more economical speech in the pulpit. The ironic parables of Jesus, in their modest earthiness and understatement, make a theological statement by their very form. They witness to the mysterious presence of God in the world, and they evoke, by their very understatement, the response of faith. In refusing to tell us too much they make a proper witness to the reign of God, the elusive but ubiquitous reality of which Jesus could speak only in parables. The preacher who keeps the sermon short and simple and relies on the commonplace makes a theological statement by the form and style of the sermon. Theologically, less is definitely more.

Liturgically, the concise homily gives way to the sacramental presence of Christ dwelling in the community, especially in its sharing of bread and wine. This is not to say that merely preaching shorter sermons makes for a sacramental community, or that lengthy preaching precludes sacramental life. In fact, a community gathered around the preacher, bonded by shared experience and language, has about it a distinctly sacramental character. Nevertheless, the concise homily is much more likely than the extended sermon to fulfill its liturgical function and to take its appropriate place in the community's liturgy of Scripture, prayer, and Sacrament. The people have their work to do, and in more cases than not the preacher, just by the time consumed by the sermon, usurps the time and energy that belong to other movements in the liturgy.

The concise homily, more than the elaborated sermon, must rely on the liturgical occasion for its power. The force of the homily comes in part from the context, as well as from the preacher's imagination or power of communication. This means that these factors must be balanced, and it also means that if the preacher simply relies upon the occasion and its liturgy to carry everything, the sermon is likely to be unsatisfactory. Some of the most ineffective and deadening preaching occurs in liturgical settings, as the preacher abdicates the crucial office of preacher and simply dwells on the liturgical occasion. That is not unlike sitting down to dinner and then spending the next hour describing the food, rather than engaging in conversation with friends or discussing matters that press upon the family. At worst, the preacher spends the whole sermon telling us what time it is: "Now on this fourth Sunday of Lent let us . . . " The gift of the liturgy to the preacher, as supportive and interpretive context, can become an all too comfortable environment, leading to homiletical sloppiness and exegetical laziness, not to mention forgetfulness of the lively and needy world outside, whose presence in prayer and, especially, in sermon, gives life to liturgy.

But this need not be the case, if the preacher makes the crucial juxtaposition: to bring together in some well-chosen words the community's formative story, revealed in Sacrament and Scripture, with the ongoing story of the people's lives. That is a pivotal moment in worship, and to ignore either the liturgical element or the community's everyday life can result in a terrible loss: Ignoring the liturgical can lead to the sermon and the preacher's personality usurping this public event in which the Word seeks to take on the form of the people's liturgical action; ignoring the community's earthly life can result in a sermon that is liturgically oriented but ultimately sterile. Storytelling is an essential means of avoiding these pitfalls while keeping the sermon concise.

Storytelling and Liturgy

We are probably closest to the essential meaning of preaching as storytelling when we understand the proper connection between preaching and liturgy. Like the authentic storyteller, whose art is always a communal activity, the preacher at her or his best is the one who gives way to the occasion and moves over for the work of the people. The concise homily at the Eucharist is the perfect example of this: For its meaning the concise sermon relies upon the whole occasion, what the church has done many times on this day—whether the weekly celebration of Sunday, or a festival day— and what this particular community is doing. Here is a hermeneutic of community: Meaning comes from Scripture by way of the sermon; however, it comes not through elaborate proofs, overblown illustrations, or force of personality, but through the connection of tradition with daily life, which is raised into liturgical action like the bread and wine at the Eucharist.

Sermons would be better if they had some of the color and drama that one sees in the religious processions of Europe and Latin America. The figure of a saint, or of the Christ, is paraded through the city's streets. Beyond all objections to graven images and unreflective piety, these parades are not lacking in humanity, color, or the willingness to embody faith in the Word made flesh. The preacher could learn from these processions, gaudy and gruesome as they sometimes are. In fact, the sermon in the midst of the people's liturgy should probably occupy the place that one of these ornate, even bloody, images has. The images are carried on the shoulders of the people; no matter how primitive, these images are works of art representing the gospel, and in the processions they are physically mingled with the secular and the mundane. Anyone who has seen a procession for the feast of Corpus Christi, or been in a Hispanic community on the day of Our Lady of Guadalupe, will know what it means for sacred and secular to merge in liturgy and art. The closest thing to the sermon at those events is the image that keeps the people reminded of what the parade is all about, even as it is carried along by the celebrating community.

What would be the shape of the concise homily that is attentive to Scripture, appropriately open to the secular world, and a good companion to the liturgy? And how might we go about revising our preparation for preaching so as to move in this direction?

Out of Print

Printed sermons are by their very form highly misleading: Apart from a living community at worship, a sermon takes on wholly different characteristics, just as a printed version of a story can seem wholly different from a version told to a circle of listeners.[32] The most consistently satisfying, and helpful, preaching I hear occurs at an early Eucharist on Thursday mornings. About twenty people meet at seven, in the choir of the church. The service lasts about thirty minutes, followed by a simple breakfast that we take turns preparing for each other. The celebrant gives a five to seven minute homily, closely connected with one of the readings for the day and with our life together. The late Rev. Nelson Thayer, who was both a priest and professor, was a frequent preacher at these services, and his disciplines of spirituality and pastoral care lent themselves to this setting for preaching. At these services, the preacher stands on the altar steps, among us and not far from the table, no notes in hand, and speaks from mind and heart about Scripture, the occasion that we are keeping, and what is happening in congregation, town, and university. These preachers are light on exegesis and most commonly introduce one secular event or image, no more, to open our eyes to the sacramental presence of God in daily life. Then we move to the Eucharist and from that to breakfast together.

Is it proximity to the Eucharist that gives these homilies their shape, requiring that they be brief and that they do not stray too far from the essential story about to be dramatized once more? Does the very repetitiousness of liturgical life free the preacher from the necessity of constant innovation and invention, so that energy goes instead to connecting, often in the simplest ways, our life with the life broken for us and now present as saving power? On this occasion, the preacher need not try to find "something to say," certainly not something new. That would be to miss the whole point of the liturgy. The people know why they are there and they are about their usual, most important work. The preacher has only to join in and to bring to this service his or her particular offering. The concise homily, given without manuscript or notes, is probably the form and style appropriate to such a eucharistic setting.

The preacher who prepares for this is not so much preparing a sermon—certainly not "getting up" a sermon—as entering into an occasion, taking his or her place among the people at their work. This calls for prayer, particularly praying through the readings for the week, rather than approaching them first of all as texts for sermons. The pastoral use of the lectionary in prayer and in the weekly rounds is part of preparation. A reassessment of attitude is essential: Am I coming to worship to give a sermon, important as that contribution is, or am I simply bringing my particular offering to add to the communal event? Is the thing here today to preach the text, or to connect Scripture with liturgy and with life, with the people's essential work, the worship of God, and with labor in home, industry, and social service?

Sermons can fail for being overprepared—especially when they are conceived as literary pieces—as well as in being underprepared. If preparation of the sermon is pursued outside the life of prayer and pastoral care and is forgetful of the liturgical cycles, energy can be wasted on making an overblown sermon that does not serve the occasion of worship. Beginning with the notion of a concise homily that will find its place at the altar is likely to move the preacher toward more focused preparation and a more discriminating choice of material. What is possible, as to form and length, at the Eucharist, and what is desirable, as to style and content, at the holy table? As we all know, there are some things, some ways of speaking, that simply do not belong at the dinner table. They are either not necessary—in families some things do not have to be said—or are out of place. The preacher who has in mind the liturgy, particularly the Eucharist, will prepare to preach in a different way.

To take other models, our sermons could have more of the qualities we seek in preaching at a marriage or a funeral, or for children. These occasions make us aware of the liturgical power and limits of the occasion itself. Even our "big" sermons would profit from coming closer to these more obviously human occasions when we are likely to move away from literary models and toward frank and down-to-earth speech.

The concise homily can be the best possible example of preaching as art and liturgy. Being less it is more, an artful act that can participate fully in the holy work of the people. In its simplicity of form and content, and in the modesty of its style, the disciplined but conversational homily can be a companion to the community's sacramental life and, at the same time, hospitable to the secular world, especially to the arts. It is to the possibilities for bringing the arts to worship that we now turn.

5
Art in the Pulpit

It is a good deal easier for most people to state an abstract idea than to describe and thus re-create some object that they actually see. But the world of the fiction writer is full of matter, and this is what the beginning fiction writers are very loath to create. They are concerned primarily with unfleshed ideas and emotions. They are apt to be reformers and to want to write because they are possessed not by a story but by the bare bones of some abstract notion. They are conscious of problems, not of people, of questions and issues, not of the texture of existence, of case histories and of everything that has a sociological smack, instead of with all those concrete details of life that make actual the mystery of our position on earth.
—Flannery O'Connor, *Mystery and Manners*

He is the Way.
Follow Him through the Land of Unlikeness;
You will see rare beasts and have unique adventures.

He is the Truth.
Seek Him in the Kingdom of Anxiety;
You will come to a great city that has expected your return for
      years.

He is the Life.
Love Him in the World of the Flesh;
And at your marriage all its occasions shall dance for joy.
      —W. H. Auden, "For the Time Being: A Christmas Oratorio"

The thesis of this book is that preaching belongs, organically, to the sacramental community, that it is a function of Christ's body, the church. From one perspective that might lead us to exclude from the pulpit what might distract from the ordered tradition of Word and Sacrament. The preacher is first and foremost the voice of Christ's body, and participation in that reality demands of the preacher, as much as of the congregation, disciplined identification with a sacred tradition, participation in a venerable liturgy, and attention to language received from the past. We might well be faulted, theologically and liturgically, if a move toward bringing the arts to homiletics forgot the specific place and purpose of preaching in the Christian tradition. At the same time that the church's liturgy opens toward the arts—and moves the preacher in that direction— the church's tradition and the gospel itself impose limits. Because of this, it is much easier to take the Christian images, literature, and liturgy to the arts than it is to bring the arts to pulpit and sanctuary.

BEYOND TRANSLATION AND ILLUSTRATION

Since the publication of *Interpretation and Imagination*, it has been necessary for me to rethink my emphasis in that book on preaching as "translation." In 1970 I wrote:

> Amid accelerating change, the preacher can no longer take for granted the strategic adequacy of his location within the world of Bible and theology. It is true that responsibility to the church as a historical community orients him toward the world of the Bible and its language, but his attendant responsibility to the church as a community moving through history lays on him the vocation of imaginative translation.[1]

Now it appears that *translation* is not an adequate word. On the one hand, such a project does not recognize the normative situation of preaching: The community understands its language first of all in relation to its sacramental identity and action. The meaning of the sermon is not so dependent upon external metaphors as the notion of translating traditional language implies. And, on the other hand, moving toward the arts with such an agenda falls short of appreciating the real affinity that exists among liturgy, the arts, and preaching. We do better to recognize the similarity between the experience of art and religious life, and the mutual dependence upon metaphor of both the artist and the sacramental community, especially its preachers.

Successfully bringing art to the pulpit is not simply a matter of shaping an artistic idiom to express a theology that we could just as well state in clear propositions, as if theology were not itself dependent upon imagination. Nor is it a matter of more thoroughly scrutinizing art in order to find better sermon illustrations, although the pulpit seems always short at that point. Rather, it is the genuine affinity between the church at worship and the arts that makes for the effective appropriation of specific works of art to liturgy and sermon. What the church does on Sunday morning is, at its best, artful, and once we see it as such the doors swing wide to drama, literature, and the visual arts.

A Liturgical and Theological Task

The preacher, both as a leader of worship and as a theologian, has a particular stake in bringing art to the pulpit. The preacher stands at that peculiar juncture where the church reiterates the faith and seeks the renewal, week after week, of its language. This means that the preacher has, in every sermon, both a liturgical and a theological task and is in a unique position to hold those together. Just at this point the arts become very important to the preacher. Nathan Scott puts it well:

> The theological act occurs in the act whereby the truth of distinctively Christian faith is set forth and clarified, but occurs also, and perhaps in certain ways even more critically, in the moment when this particular faith is required to define and understand itself in relation to the general fund of wisdom about what is important in human life on earth.[2]

Here is the appropriate context for bringing the arts to the pulpit: We must recognize our common reliance upon metaphor and appreciate the artists' gift for showing us, in their inimitable ways, what is important in human life on earth.

Accordingly, this chapter intends to consider, first, the homiletical and liturgical implications of literature, drama, and film, and then to make concrete suggestions for bringing those popular arts to Christian worship. No one has laid better groundwork for this than R. E. C. Browne, who was a pastor and preacher in Manchester, England. Canon Browne reminds us that preaching is an art, and points the preacher toward the arts because of his belief that "the mode of divine revelation determines the mode of [all] preaching." He continues: "There can be no great preaching whenever the question 'Is there a knowledge of reality which can neither be perceived nor expressed in propositional form?' is unasked or left unanswered."[3]

It is art, he says, that can both tolerate and express the ambiguous, that can live with chaos but somehow also order it. The artist cannot separate her or his person from the work of art: "Painting is not merely what a painter does when she is at the canvas with the brush in her hand; the painting arises largely through what she does when she is not painting or thinking about painting."[4] In the same way, preachers cannot separate their lives from their sermons. The vocation of the preacher, Browne shows, is closely analogous to that of the dedicated artist, both seeking to express the inexpressible and relying for this upon both discipline and imagination. The church and its preachers live on the gifts of the imagination and for the creative moment of illumination.

The church—as one can clearly see in liturgy and architecture—is no stranger to art, and those who preach have a particular stake in the arts. Can we not assert that the Christ embodied in the sacramental community continues to seek embodiment, and in unlikely forms? Can we doubt that the arts might offer themselves, or be offered by a discerning interpreter, as vehicles of God's Word revealed in Christ and present in the Holy Spirit? Is it not true that there are many artists who are unaware of their roles as allies of the gospel? Aren't they our allies simply because what we preach is the Word incarnate, a Word that is being interpreted to us in every generation by the power of the Spirit? This book grounds homiletics in the second person of the Trinity, the Word incarnate, but we are opened toward the arts no less by the creator of all things and by the life-giving Spirit.

Humanity and Art

We may find the word *art* intimidating, but to be human is to be an artist. *Art*, in its root meaning, refers to the human ability to acquire skills and to use those skills creatively. Homo sapiens is an artisan who makes tools and builds culture: At its very root art has to do with common materials, with fashioning what is at hand, with earth. The human artisan learns not merely the skills of survival but is constantly fashioning signs and symbols, the essential tools of survival in human community. Homo sapiens uses language, paints pictures on the walls of caves, tells stories, refines liturgies, and transcends even death by the power of imagination. In all its varied forms, art is as common to the modern human family everywhere as it was among those primitive bands gathered around their fires. We give a double meaning to the word *culture*: It refers to the very fabric of social interaction and, in its more narrow meaning, to the arts.

While the word *art* may be applied variously to making a pie, sculpting marble, writing a novel, or building a house, we recognize the special abilities of some persons to express aesthetically our deepest feelings and highest values, our common longings and difficult questions. We reserve use of the title "artist" for these persons. Even when we say of the fine carpenter, "He's an artist!" or of the accomplished manager, "She has that down to a fine art," we do this by reference to the more specific meaning that we have come to give the word. At the same time, however, *art* most likely means, at root, "to fit." Those who make things fit, who bring order out of chaos by fitting together a story, or a landscape in canvas and oil, who somehow compose a symphony or put life on the stage—all those have a right to be called artists.

The similarity between this understanding of art and the homiletic set forth in this book is obvious. The preacher, too, aims at material expression of what is virtually inexpressible, the situation in which all human life stands. This understanding—that humanity and art are inseparable—offers a proper context in which to consider bringing specific arts to the pulpit. This in no way diminishes what we call "the arts," but it reminds us that when we are about the things that matter most to human beings—enhancing our environment, passing on to others what we have found most important, making sense out of our experiences, expressing our deepest feelings of truth and beauty, or simply doing the work of daily living—we are never far from what is signified by the word *art*. There is no reason for any person, however untutored in art history or literary criticism, to feel that he or she is a stranger here. Just as all of us have a stake in human creativity, each of us is, in some sense of the word, an artist, and only by realizing that can we fully appreciate those whom we recognize in some special way as worthy of the designation.

Artists are especially skilled in symbol-making. Keen eyes and ears, deft hands, sensitive spirits, gifts of language and agility—this list could go on—let them put into paint and paragraphs, motion and music, memorized lines and celluloid film, what they have experienced and imagined of being human. In their works, feeling takes material form, as painting, play, motion picture, dance, poem. The function of these forms in the human community is symbolic: The work of art is intended to produce in the viewer or hearer something of the experience that moved the artist to make it. Following this understanding of the nature of the symbolic, one could say that a symbol is the residue and the catalyst of experience.[5] Human society is able to hold together and to continue because one person, or one generation, communicates its experience to another by symbol-making. The artist is the one especially gifted in making these symbols by which we tell each other what it is to be human.

Storytelling is a particularly important form of art. Probably the most common means of symbolizing, it occurs in all human societies and requires nothing more than one human being speaking to another. Storytelling is something we can all do, and it is an art to which we all readily respond. People everywhere, young and old, sophisticated and uneducated, know innately how to tell and hear stories, and in all human cultures the storyteller plays an essential role. The phenomenon of the story is crucial for this book: The gospel itself takes the form of a story, and that fact leads us to literature, drama, and cinema as sources of models and material for preaching.

Every human being and every human community lives by story. Without a constant artful weaving and hearing of tales, neither our personal lives nor our communities could hold together. Any person who is functioning reasonably well day-to-day and living successfully as part of one or more communities—family, church, town—is doing a great deal of imaginative work, mostly in the form of story-making, whether or not he or she is aware of it. What happens to me or to my group today must be somehow related to what happened yesterday and to what I am expecting tomorrow. I am most likely to make those connections, links that turn experience into meaning, by weaving a cohesive story that makes things fit.

It once struck me as strange that my family began the day by reading the obituary page of *The Lincoln County Republican* in a small

Oklahoma town where everyone seemed to be related to everyone else, in one way or another. My grandparents seemed never quite satisfied until the persons mentioned on the black-bordered page had been fitted into the skein of blood and land into which their own lives were woven. "So-and-so was related to so-and-so, who lived at this place or that, and she married such-and-such, who lived two miles north of our place. . . . " It was, it now seems, a way of locating themselves in that landscape, and it suggests our way of locating ourselves, too, in relation to our own past and to the various communities in which we live. These same people, who had time for sitting on the porch on summer evenings and for going to lengthy funerals, used those occasions to rehearse over and over again the stories that bound them to family and friends, to history and geography.

It was years later that I began to understand what storytelling was to them: the symbolic transformation of experience into meaning. As Boris Pasternak put it, "Man does not die in a ditch like a dog, but at home in history."[6] Sitting over the still-laden table on the evening of a funeral in rural America, one can get a glimpse of people accomplishing that, saving even death from meaninglessness. Stories are told *on* as well as about the deceased, as if the people need to show the worst as well as the best side, or to act out in laughter a ritual of forgiveness and final reconciliation. What is the function of this storytelling in such a community if not to redeem from meaninglessness the life of the person now dead and, following disruption, to make it all fit again? As John Cheever once put it, "Art is the triumph over chaos."[7] This is accomplished by telling stories to laugh and cry over, stories that weave that one life, by means of comic and tragic art and a kind of folk forgiveness, into the ongoing life of a people. We can laugh at her foibles: We can hope, too, that our failings will receive kindly treatment. We can, here on the very evening of his burial—which can only make us aware of our own—keep him present with us by telling about the time he built a new house in the middle of the Depression, or despite hard times spoiled his first grandson.

Individuals, like communities, live by story. Any man or woman who responds to life each day with a more or less steady sense of well-being owes that in no small part to the art of storytelling, for storytelling is our primary means of integrating experiences. We do not do well with disconnected experience: If we are to be healthy each scene has to be related somehow to the larger scenario, each episode to the whole, our lines to the entire play. In the movie *Last Tango in Paris*, a displaced couple agree to meet in a hotel room, to tell each other nothing about themselves, not even their names. They will simply enjoy these afternoons without any of the complications of getting to know each other. It doesn't work. Even passionate sexual experience becomes increasingly intolerable when severed from coherent life stories. Who they are—people who have lived in other times and places and with other people—keeps breaking in as pieces of their biographies emerge. The human need for meaning intrudes.

What this means for individual health as well as for the maintenance of social structures is apparent: The stories we tell, forget, or avoid contribute to our well-being or to illness. In psychotherapy it can take years for people to get in touch with their health-giving stories and to exorcise the destructive ones. Although the realm of dreams remains mysterious, it is clear that in dreaming we do a great deal of imaginative story-work, in which the conflicts of the subconscious seek resolution. In the church, much of a pastor's time is given to providing people the freedom to do this all-important symbolizing, to weave what is happening into the fabric of a viable life story. Anyone who has been through crisis, or who has simply come home from school or work bursting to tell someone what happened, knows the importance of story-making. It is not possible to live a fully human life without this daily symbolic work that transforms experience into meaning. As Michael Novak put it: "Action . . . lacking a story to give it significance seems pointless. Why bother to do anything at all? . . . Not to have a story to live out is to experience nothingness: the primal formlessness of human life below the threshold of narrative structuring."[8] No wonder, then, that our earliest forebears decorated the walls of their caves, or that week in and week out people bring their joys and sorrows to the place of Word and Sacrament. Life is more than one damn thing after another: Those who tell stories and celebrate the Eucharist make it so.

The Church as Art

If it is true that individuals and communities could not hold together without continuous creativity, this is especially true of the church. Art, imagination, story, symbol, drama—these are the church's territory. As far as the churches may have drifted into managerial models of ministry, a pedestrian moralism as the profile of religious life, and what Nathan Scott calls "positivism,"[9] still the church through its long history has played the artist. This is much more than the church's historic patronage of the arts. Rather, it is the nature of faith to live by imagination, to rely upon material expression of what is deeply known but difficult to say.

Start with the Bible. It is easy to forget that the Bible is, whatever else we may say about it, a storybook. We may divide it into chapter and verse, parse its poetry, turn its tragicomedy into texts, and make so much of its jots and tittles that we cannot hear the stories as stories, but the Bible remains, nonetheless, a storybook. The Hebrew Scriptures tell the saga of a wandering people and their heroines and heroes. Even when Israel's teachers and prophets turn to non-narrative writing, it is by reference to this story that they speak wisdom, admonish to just action, and sing their songs of praise. At the heart of the Hebrew Scriptures is a story of deliverance from slavery that was told and retold, orally, from generation to generation. The storytellers of Israel, its preachers and teachers, kept alive the story and all the narrative and poetry attached to it. It was out of these saving stories that God's people lived. We can only try to imagine how different our religious communities would be if we had no written canon, only the art of the storyteller and singer.

The New Testament, too, is at heart a story comprising many stories, and the Gospels, members of a unique genre, are carefully crafted works of art that form the New Testament's core. The narrative of Jesus and of his first followers becomes the context for the stories he told, and the church's larger kerygmatic story encompasses all. Here again it is speech: Jesus did not write; the church's witness to him was oral; and to this day we *hear* the Word of God in a human voice. To repeat, of all scriptural texts, the parables are probably closest to the words of the historical Jesus;

they are stories that Jesus told while face to face with his opponents, stories in the poetic language of a keen observer of daily life.

On Sunday mornings people congregate to listen to the Bible, even to reverence it, sometimes by means of lavish liturgical action. The people may stand for the Gospel, burn incense around the book, or pay special attention to it in some way. The reader may stumble; criticism or common sense may call into question the writer's accuracy, relevance, or moral maturity; the language may seem antique, the sentiment quaint. But by some trick, some sleight of hand, or out of habit, we keep on listening as if everything depended upon this book. This is, whatever else it may be, an act of imagination. The man who teaches our children sixth grade or the woman who does my taxes reads an account of a great flood, or from a letter written to people in Rome two millennia ago, and announces: "The Word of God." We may attempt to justify this by theological argument, resort to simplistic notions of divine inspiration, or speak of the Holy Spirit's miraculous work. But to exclude from such accounting sheer artistry, poetry, and the evocative and mysterious power of language—that would be to underestimate the stake of faith in imagination.

The Artless Church

Much that is problematic in the life of the church today is due to the loss of imagination, particularly in the use of Scripture. Scripture is read in most liturgies, acknowledged as authoritative for both individuals and the community, and is present in many Christian homes. But when imagination fails the Bible can become divisive, confusing, and so controversial as to usurp the church's time and energy. One pastor said: "Sometimes I want to stop my people from reading the Bible; it can be more trouble than it is worth."

To whatever else we may attribute the difficulties we have with the Bible, the literal mind is no small part of the problem. The moment I begin to turn story into history, prophetic poetry into pat prediction, the apocalyptic and eschatological language of faith's struggle and longing toward the relative and limited concerns of our cultural biases and political ideologies, the Bible becomes the precise opposite of what we claim for it, the Word of the one, holy, and transcendent God. It becomes a book that I commandeer, divide into easily manipulated snippets, and use for the pragmatic agenda of my particular group. This may stem, as chapter 2 suggested, from the privatizing of hermeneutics, but it springs also from a failure of imagination.

Whatever else the Bible is, it is literature, and literary experience is literary experience, whether one is reading Scripture or *The Catcher in the Rye*.[10] The idea of *Holy* Scripture may be unfortunate, to the degree that in gilding its pages and elevating it to infallible authority—a claim not made by Scripture itself[11]—we may cut ourselves off from experiencing it as literature, from entering into its stories as a child would, from meeting its characters as vivid women and men, and from hearing the poetry of prophet and psalmist. Add to this attributed weight the many agendas we bring to the Bible—the mores of our group, the preaching of sermons, institutional needs, and so forth—and it becomes increasingly unlikely that we will be able to read the Bible as a storybook with anything like the imagination of its writers or original hearers. This book of saga and legend, of adventure and poetry, of personal letter and inventive testimony, comprising the range of literary genres, is turned into a collection of texts for preaching, ammunition for this or that moral position, polite advice for good living.

Take two examples. A preacher takes a parable of Jesus, the story of the father and his two sons (Luke 15:11-32), and from it constructs a three-point sermon on how far we have drifted from what is important, how much we need to repent, and what a welcome there will be for us in the church and/or heaven: a not uncommon sermonic treatment of this parable. If we came to this parable as story we would probably come out with a quite different form and content, something closer to earth and more gracious. Or in the story of the magi (Matt. 2:1-12), for Epiphany, the preacher fixes on a geographical detail, "they went back another way," and in a sermon on conversion loses much of the wonderful tale of people following a star and, even in the presence of cynical power, bowing to a child. A more imaginative approach to Scripture, tutored by the arts, would yield different models and material.

LITERATURE IN THE PULPIT

Even the way we study the Bible can block experience of it. C. S. Lewis describes a group of literary aficionados, the sort that used to meet on Tuesday afternoon to discuss the book of the month. Such a circle might meet to analyze the book, to probe the meaning of its title and abstruse symbolism, or perhaps for no other reason than to be in fashion. Even if the preoccupation were with criticism, there is little room for identifying with the characters or engaging their situation. But, says Lewis, while this non-engagement is going on, "real literary experience may be occurring in a back bedroom where a small boy is reading *Treasure Island* under the bed-clothes by the light of an electric torch."[12] Literature, including the Bible, is available to us, before it is anything else, as literature—story and poem and epic, image and turn of phrase, letters and Gospels, parables and proverbs—that can seize the imagination and transform consciousness. That experience is the common ground of Scripture and imaginative literature, and it is there that we begin in bringing the writers of our day to the pulpit.

A person reading should be intensely alive. There is a quality of vitality, a heightened attentiveness that comes from the experience of literature. If preaching is, as someone said, two-thirds listening, then the preacher can learn much from intensely reading and "listening" to literature. Among the arts, literature has the capacity to engage us totally, to carry us away, so that body, mind, and soul are given to the experience of other people, to times and places that invite us away from the taken-for-granted and into the mysterious heights and depths of human existence. In the case of Scripture, it is this giving of ourselves, this deep engagement, that opens the Bible to us as a living book, in whose human voices we hear the voice of the holy. If we do not engage the Bible as literature but remain bent on breaking it into isolated bits and pieces that we call "texts," then it becomes not unlike one of those beached whales, with people standing about curiously poking and taking pictures, while the animal dies on the sand. Captain Ahab, by contrast, has a far deeper knowledge of Moby Dick, tossed and wounded as he was in the great whale's company.

Reading the Bible

Whatever else may be said of the preacher, she or he is constantly involved with a book. Ordination vows call for this, and one of the strongest expectations of people who listen to sermons is that the preacher will read, meditate upon, and interpret the book. Preaching is, for good or ill, a bookish vocation, and wherever else the calling to preach may connect with contemporary literature, they certainly meet on the common ground of reading. When it comes to exegesis for preaching, one of the elements most missing is this experience of literature. Anyone who has read even a love story, or feared to turn the next page of a thriller, knows the power of literature, the intensity that can come from ink on paper. As a first step toward imaginative preaching could we bring to Scripture something of the experience of reading a good book? If somehow we could move from using Scripture to getting lost in it, to a deeper engagement of human sensibility, preaching would be well served.

It is not necessary to say that literature and lectionary are the same in order to mark out the common terrain of faith and fiction. Some have suggested that the arts take the place of liturgical life for many people today. While that may be so, it is certainly not presupposed here. But, in the experience of literature—a child lost in *Treasure Island*[13]—we see something essential to the apprehension of canonical literature and to its interpretation in the life of the church. It is where people are intensely alive, having a "good read," that the familiar language of Scripture and liturgy comes to life.

This means that the more we can come to the Bible as we come to the novel and short story—open, ready to go through the looking glass, willing to be surprised and carried into the mystery, unafraid to feel, to let language have its own way, suspending critical judgment and giving way to playful imagination—the more likely we are to experience Scripture as the Word of God for us now. Two of the principal benefits of reading novels and stories are quickened imagination and heightened sensibility, and these spill over into exegesis. Whatever one's view of canon, exegesis closer to a child's reading of Robert Lewis Stevenson could only stimulate preaching.

Walter Wink has developed a method of Bible study that seeks to merge historical-critical study and what we are calling here an experience of literature. The model of taking the text apart and analyzing it in every detail—to the neglect of seeing the images, identifying with the human faces, and following the dramatic action—is inadequate for preaching and teaching in a community of faith. The whole purpose in having a canon is for the nurturing and guidance of the community; the canon's essential purpose is hardly to be a target of academic study. Hence Wink wants a more personally engaged and imaginative exegesis.[14]

Other Biblical scholars with a special concern for preaching— Leander Keck, Fred Craddock, James Sanders—have also urged a more attentive, deeper listening, a willingness to play with the words and to be played with by the language, so that the images and stories have their own way with us. Further, revisions in the lectionary that leave the stories whole rather than dissecting them into texts, particularly in the Hebrew Scriptures, move us toward seeing the Scriptures as literature. All of this augurs well for preaching and the literary arts, by marking out at this basic level a common reliance upon imagination that, before making a move toward interpretation, listens, waits, and sees. This kind of reading is training in metaphorical understanding and communication, of the sort that John Crossan describes:

> When a metaphor contains a radically new vision of world it gives absolutely no information until after the hearer has entered into it and experienced it from inside itself. In such cases the hearer's first reaction may be to refuse to enter into the metaphor and one will seek to translate it immediately into the comfortable normalcy of one's ordinary linguistic world. . . . One must risk entrance before one can experience its validity.[15]

The quality that distinguishes the preaching of such diverse contemporaries as Frederick Buechner, James Forbes, and Barbara Brown Taylor comes from this intense engagement with the images and narratives of Scripture.

Linking preaching to literature is not to suggest that homiletics is just one more of the arts. The work of preaching is a pastoral office, related in a special way to the sacred canon of a community of faith, and exercised on the authority of the church. Preaching occurs, as we have seen, in worship, and it aims at the nurture and perpetuation of a liturgically formed community. These distinctions, it is true, may be unduly emphasized so as to set the preacher apart from the world and even at a distance from the arts. Preaching is a unique art, owing to its function in the community and in relation to the canon. At the same time, however, the nature of both community and canon predisposes homiletics toward the arts.

The one collection of sermons that I have all my students read is Frederick Buechner's *The Magnificent Defeat*,[16] for the simple reason that Buechner, of all the preachers I know, exemplifies bringing together the preacher's world of canon and community with culture. Buechner's sermons reveal a man whose imagination is furnished with the Bible's stories and images and who, at the same time, dwells in the stories, memories, and dreams of humankind. It is the coalescence of the Bible's images with Buechner's personal experience and with culture that gives these sermons power, even in print. To take one example, Buechner pictures himself in bed early in the morning, somewhere between waking and sleeping. With the first light of a new day—it seems to him the light of creation—peeping through the window, he hears a voice: "Let there be Buechner."[17] That is where preaching and literature meet, where the Bible is apprehended with imagination and its stories connect with the realities of being human.

A Light to Read By

Reading with an eye to preaching is reading for the story itself, and only then with a theological and homiletical agenda, a kind of double reading. "Theology is a light to read by," Stuart Henry used to say, a perspective on literature. But the story is the thing. As we sit down with a novel, or a book of short stories or poetry, how shall we go about this double reading?

To begin, let us be engaged by the story itself. At this stage let us *not* think of reading as doing theological or homiletical work. Henry suggested theology is a light to read by, to help us see more clearly, but not a light of which we would be constantly aware. A sure way not to experience literature is to go at it with a constantly beaming theological searchlight. Next, at a second stage, let us now think of reading as doing the work of theology, in a way not unlike trying to hear what is behind the conversations on our pastoral rounds, looking under the language, going more deeply into what we observe.

This, in daily living and in our pastoral work, does what Paul Tillich saw as the contemporary theological task, to see at the depths of all human experience the question of God.[18]

The idea, then, is to read as theologians and preaching pastors, but also to read as if we were not. This is analogous to cultivating the talent for listening to a sermon as an unschooled, needy person even though we have been schooled in theology and homiletical criticism. Reading will be much less interesting if the question of God is not there, less rich if we do not bring our pastoral concerns with us. But the story is the thing, and giving it time and space to happen to us is the primary agenda. As Wallace Stevens said, the aim is to see "the very thing and nothing else."[19]

Metaphor and Illustration

John Crossan distinguishes between illustration and metaphor: I use illustration; metaphor uses me.[20] Whether it is a biblical text or a short story, vitality comes from the preacher's being caught up and compelled by the action and images. This is apparent in two quite specific homiletical techniques. One is cueing, the method by which a preacher, following a manuscript, steps outside the typescript for a moment and "cues" herself or himself, by a single word or phrase, to tell a story. With this technique, the story has its way with the teller. Almost without exception, sermons come alive where this little cue—a word or phrase in a box sketched on the page—frees the preacher to follow the story. Delivery becomes more animated and communication is heightened as the story actually happens, the image appears, enfleshed once more in the storyteller.[21]

The other technique is the common homiletical practice of setting a single image or story early in the sermon, fixing it well in the imagination of the preacher and congregation, projecting it up on the wall of the imagination and asking all to take time to look at it. Once this is done, when the congregation and preacher are in the power of the story or image, the preacher can move to interpretation in connection with Scripture, liturgy, and what is happening in the community.

Each of these suggests the power of the image to take over the preacher and through him or her the congregation. It is this power to enthrall that is the essential power of story, and it is the corrective to what Phillips Brooks called "the habit of criticism," the tendency to put everything in our power, that is, to turn everything into illustration.[22] For the preacher, this is the point of unmistakable kinship with literature, where the metaphors have their own way. It is what one sees in such conductors as Seiji Ozawa, who can lead a great orchestra to create music because the music comes not only from notes that Beethoven wrote down but also from the conductor's embodying, being possessed by, the music. There is one scene in the documentary on Ozawa shown on Public Television in which the conductor in his study is going over a score. As he stands at his work table, the music lies open before him. As he pores over the text and adds his own notes to the margins, the music of Beethoven, as if coming from his own imagination, overarches the scene. Is not that what we hope for, to pay close attention to the tradition, while bringing to it something from our own heart and mind, so that the music can be heard? Is that too much to hope for in exegesis of Scripture? Or in reliving literary experience in the pulpit?

A Second Reading

The proper sequence, then, in the preparation of sermons is personal engagement with the literature followed by a second reading, as it were. Criticism, theological reflection, application to the issues of the day—all depend upon this prior experience. As Amos Wilder puts it, "Before the message, there must be the vision, before the sermon the hymn, before the prose the poem."[23] In chapter 3 we sketched an outline of the preacher's weekly engagement with Scripture. That process is pertinent here. In sum it is this: Monday, read and meditate on the pericopes; Tuesday and Wednesday, read commentaries and pertinent theological sources; Thursday, begin writing the sermon by articulating the main idea or image and finding a design organic to that; Friday, finish writing the sermon by devising an instrument for the pulpit (typescript, notes, a "map," chart, etc.).[24] All of this is built on the *cantus firmus* of Monday's engagement and is developed in the context of going about the work of a pastor.

Reading literature with an eye to preaching parallels roughly this sequence. The pastor who is alive to the life of a parish and theologically aware will read by a certain light. Pastoral concerns and issues of the day will probably lead the reader's eye to rest on certain images. I have learned to make brief notes in pencil at the back of the book, a kind of running index to the pages where the story has connected with Scripture and the life of the parish. This index is no more than a list of words and phrases, perhaps a line or two from a passage—just enough to enable the reader to find this later. These quick, telegraphic notes do not distract unduly from staying with the story, and they facilitate a second, more reflective reading. This simple index makes future reference easy, when the preacher is trying to recover, months or years later, a lively image or compelling character.

There are two obvious possibilities for bringing literature to the pulpit: overview and excerpt. The preacher can tell the whole story from the perspective of one who sees it whole and can summarize in such a way as to reveal a central issue, idea, or question. This is somewhat difficult to accomplish and usually not does not result in conveying the flavor of the story as well as the second method. By excerpting—isolating a scene, character, even a single paragraph—the preacher allows one small piece of the story to carry the whole. A *pericope*, in the precise meaning of the word, is a bit of text cut out of the story and framed in such a way as to reveal the whole. In excerpting it is important to allow the concrete images and specific language of the piece to speak in their own way and, at the same time, to keep the whole in view. These are, of course, the rules of any good exegesis: As we try to listen to three verses from Mark's Gospel, we try to keep the larger Gospel, and indeed the gospel message itself, in view while paying close attention to this particular narrative or scene.

It is also possible to trace a theme or a question through various parts of the story. Such a thematic approach is more difficult to handle, often resulting in a sermon that could as well be made without the particular story. Helmut Thielicke said that almost all preaching is "textual/thematic," in varying mixtures. In preaching from literature, the trick is to pay close attention to the "text" while bringing to it, in an artful way that does justice to the genre, the themes and questions that our pastoral situation and the Gospel provide.

THE MOVIES: SERMON AND CINEMA AS PARABLE

Today angels cannot appear as they once appeared. . . . They will come in other ways. . . . In the Bible angels are not at all religious. They almost never confront us in the specially religious contexts of worship, cultus, religious language, or theological reflections. . . . Angels encounter people where, to our way of thinking, we would never expect to find messengers of God.
                    —Claus Westermann, *God's Angels Need No Wings*

You cannot tell people what to do, you can only tell them parables; and that is what art really is, particular stories of particular people and experiences.
                    —W. H. Auden, cited in M. K. Spears,
                                        The Poetry of W. H. Auden

The moviemaker can show us a human face ten feet tall. As with the novelist, who may spend hundreds of pages on what happened to one person somewhere, sometime, this is a profoundly Christian thing to do. Through the camera the moviemaker has the capacity to contemplate the world, to pay attention to the single individual, the concrete particular, to linger over one small episode in a family's history or to bring before our eyes an entire city going dark or waking to throbbing life. The camera can frame the individual, the parochial, and the provincial, and thus moviemaking is, at least potentially, a quintessentially Christian art.

There are at least three reasons to say this. First, the Christian religion holds out for the worth of each human being. God revealed in Jesus of Nazareth is God blessing and raising to infinite value every human life. We find human beings and what happens to them interesting as such, but the heritage of Christian civilization in Christian teaching, particularly the doctrine of the incarnation, is the context in which many novelists tell their stories and many moviemakers train their cameras. For example, in the opening scene of *La Dolce Vita*, a helicopter swings a statue of the Christ above modern Rome, the dome of St. Peter's looming in the background; this is a metaphor of modern cinematic art. Moviemakers have been tremendously affected, though this is often unconscious, by Christian tradition and especially by its emphasis on the human and the particular. Ironically, Hollywood owes quite a debt to Bethlehem.

Second, the camera has a unique capacity to hold before our eyes the world as it is, and yet from a transcendent perspective. Writers achieve this also, but in bringing before our very eyes the world, we may say, as God sees it, the motion picture is unrivaled. Christianity, at its best, does not blink before the world or shun it, but in the face of a candid apprehension celebrates the Eucharist and preaches the gospel. Like the movies, Christianity has a transcendent perspective, but the faith of the cross does not avert its gaze from anything human, and so it can welcome the camera.

Third, there is similarity between the art of cinema and a primary form of Christian communication, the parable. The parabolic teaching of Jesus assumes the power of the image, the promise of human redemption in *seeing*. Motion pictures, in a way not unlike the art of the parable, show us this very world, with an artistry that helps us see more.

If we are to make such claims for cinema, it can be only on the basis of critical discrimination. There are movies and there are movies. Even those who sell motion pictures have had to agree on a system for rating their product. Many films are no more than distracting entertainment, and as many have little purpose beyond the box office. Harvey Cox's critique rings all too true: "All art illuminates the mystery of human existence. But just as not all paintings or statues are art, likewise, very few of the thousands of films produced each year are art. Very few of today's films convey fresh visions of reality. Most convey sentimental cliches."[25] Cox's criticism is, however, in the context of his assertion that cinema is the characteristic art form of the midtwentieth century: "All other art forms, from ballet to ceramics, live in the film age and are influenced by it."[26]

Film and Liturgy

Film is a powerful part of what Cox calls "the consciousness industry." Movies do not just mirror culture; they form our spiritual outlook and are probably without peer in shaping the thought and style of the rising generation. Along with other forms of entertainment and advertising, filmmaking actually molds consciousness of what it is to be a human being in a particular society today. This must account for the caution with which many Christians have gone to the movies. We are aware of the enormous power of this medium.

The motion picture theater is a unique place: In darkness and anonymity the viewer sits for two or three hours in uninterrupted communication with a larger-than-life series of images and enveloping sound. The camera is unblinking, capable of showing the greatest detail. At the same time, the moviemaker can easily distort space and time. But as easily as the camera may be used to manipulate and to trick us, the screenwriter, director, camera crew, and editor can help us to see more clearly the people and things around us. The camera's selective eye focuses, enlarges, distorts, and presents images to us without regard to clock or calendar, all in the interest of showing us what we might not otherwise notice.

Going to the movies—as distinguished from sitting in one's home watching a film on television—is a communal experience. The response of the audience is a significant part of the experience. The theater provides a unique intimacy: To sit in a darkened theater before the unfolding images of human joy and sorrow, ecstasy and pain, to look at the face of loneliness and into the depths of evil, make of an audience a kind of congregation. Facing unabridged reality together sometimes creates intense anxiety, which comes out most often as defensive talking.

The parallels with liturgy are obvious. Liturgy is multimedia, appeals strongly to the senses, and combines both corporate and private experience. The Eucharist, especially, accomplishes what Cox sees the cinema as capable of accomplishing, that is, the recombining of "the commonplace," in this case the "superficial trivia" of bread and wine, to move us toward a unified experience. The central mystery of the Christian faith is a matter of food and drink, putting those who celebrate the Eucharist more in the camp of the ironic and secular filmmakers than in that of the producers of such heroic religious epics as *Ben Hur* or *King of Kings*. Christians at worship at the end of this century continue, in the face of overwhelming forces, to break bread and share a cup. They are, if we follow Cox, acting out what he sees portrayed in contemporary film. The Italians in particular, Cox argues, know what it is to live in a land of empty vessels: "Modern neurotic Romans drive their hopped-up Fiats and copulate in sterile modern apartments, but all of it within the somber shadow of St. Peter's." These filmmakers are able "to affirm both our modernity and our humanity in an age of radical secularity."[27] This could as well be a description of Christians, all too aware of the polluted, armed-to-the-teeth, sick and starving world around them, and of the divisions among themselves, as they gather around the holy table.

Sermon and Cinema as Parable

Preaching, too, focuses on the particular, naming the very thing, the person, not just telling us about "love" but showing us specific persons—a man smelling of Clorox cleaning the bathroom, a woman inviting her estranged neighbor for coffee—who in their concreteness bring us to the moment of illumination. The commonplaces of every day make the scenario of grace, as much in our preaching today as in the parables of Jesus. Sallie McFague writes: "The gospel was identified not with a teaching or a religious experience but an action or history played out in the particular stories of individuals." She goes on to quote William Lynch: "What we need is the restoration of a confidence in the fundamental power of the finite and limited concretions of our human life."[28]

Preachers, then, are not wasting time when they go to the movies, an art form not far from Word and Sacrament. Many of the people who come to church on Sunday will have seen a movie that week, and some of those films afford the preacher real opportunity for interpreting our times and communicating the gospel. As an example, consider the work of Stephen Spielberg as cinematic parable.

If a parable is an image of the world presented in such a way as to shatter the familiar, taken-for-granted world, then Spielberg is a very good case in point. The teller of parables, working from a vision of a transformed cosmos—for us, the reign of God—meets us on the ground of the normal, the predictable, the prosaic, only to turn everything on its head and announce a new world. The ordinary becomes the vehicle of the extraordinary, the recalcitrant order of things the occasion for the advent of the new and the transformation of all things.

Some of Spielberg's films suggest a worldview, the hope of innocence, peace, justice, nonviolence. But how does he tell stories that serve such a vision? Take *Close Encounters of the Third Kind* as an example. The subject matter itself evokes some foreboding: We normally think of creatures from outer space as invaders. Spielberg plays on this, so that what we expect does in fact seem to be happening: We connect the technology of spaceships with the threat of weapons and aggressive foreigners. The gigantic spaceship comes thundering to earth, and ever so slowly its hatch opens and the ramp descends. But what comes down the gangway to meet us is not at all a bloodthirsty stranger from outer space, but a gentle creature most like a human fetus. Here is complete surprise, a turning of the tables that disarms our paranoid fear of the stranger, reminds us of our common humanity, and opens toward new possibilities for human interaction.

Spielberg's stories take place in the most recognizable places: at home, in a suburban environment, among children at play and riding bicycles, with nature in view. These are stories of the world as we know it, to which Spielberg comes in such as way to meet us just there, to disorient us from entrenched attitudes, and to open us toward new possibilities. In this connection, Gerhard Ebeling has said that "the art of the parable is none other than that of bringing the hearer face to face with what it is to be human and thereby to make clear what it means for God to draw near."[29] This is accomplished, Wilder says, by marrying the deep questions of our lives to "ordinariness and secularity."[30] Even the futuristic themes of Spielberg can have these qualities, a recognizable humanity and secularity, and some of this power.

Going to the movies with an eye to preaching the gospel, our concern is less with questions of pornography and profanity than with authenticity: Does the film lead us to a moment of recognition? Though there are obviously limits to this, we would do well to take a cue from Jesus who, in his parables, was relatively indifferent to the moral rectitude of his characters. The story is the thing. The first concern in telling a joke—though there are obviously limits here as well—is whether it makes us laugh.

A Word from Below

Whatever the theological, pastoral, or prophetic agendas the preacher may bring to the sermon, those are best served by a technique not unlike the potentially parabolic art of the moviemaker. The preacher need not address modern culture from above: To address from below, from within, would be the way of the parable.

Put another way, if approached artfully and in the context of lit-urgy, culture can address itself. Jesus hardly speaks of God, and when he speaks of the reign of God he does not expect his hearers to have a fully and perfectly developed vision of the realm, as if this could be put in so many words. As a teller of parables, he does not speak of these things from the perspective of the divine. Rather, in his parables he begins at the other end: Here is a picture of our life together and the common world we share. Have we eyes to see God, and what God demands of us, in that?

Do the movies have a unique capacity to place us in a setting that asks questions, by placing the very world we are making before our eyes? Though *Hollywood* has become an adjective meaning unreal, slick, happy-ever-after, cinema does take pictures of the actual world. As Cox puts it: "Let cinema be cinema, let it hold be-fore us the shattered pieces of our everyday world, until they take a shape that allows us to see ourselves as we are, and therefore, per-haps to see beyond."[31] In these mundane images lies the prophetic possibility of movies, as of preaching.

A graduate student of mine, a seasoned pastor, told me that for the first few years of his present ministry to an affluent congregation of urbane sophisticates he had tried to make his people "more spir-itual." "Now," he said, "I am trying to live my people's lives with them and to help us all see the presence and demands of God in the depth of the life we live." That is probably the actual situation of the great prophets and preachers, and such a point of view makes the preacher a kind of well-aimed camera moving about town.

There is room, also, for theological critique of the movies. We can assert, at the same time, the theological competence of the secular and the necessity for theological criticism. Contemporary vision and Christian tradition will be most fruitfully brought to-gether through dialogue. Since theology itself is a matter of constant revision, the theologian, as well as the moviemaker, stands to gain from this dialogue.[32]

Rubrics

• Still within smelling distance of the popcorn, your companion asks as you are leaving the theater, "Well, what did you think of that?" You don't want to discuss the movie, not now. If this has happened to you, you know the power of film to carry you away to a place beyond analysis or criticism. The movie is the thing. So just go to the show like the kid at the gas station. At this point don't worry about cinematic criticism and cogent analysis.

• When you get home, if the film has moved you, write down the names of the characters, brief descriptions of settings, and other details. Was one scene especially compelling (this may come to you later)? If so, make a few notes on the action; try to recall the details. Does some of the dialogue stay with you? Write it down now.

• What problems, questions, and issues does the film raise for you? (The problem is often the homiletical opportunity.) Does the movie evoke something of the biblical tradition, or is there explicit connection with church, liturgical season, theology? Make some notes.

• As you read the lections for the week and mark the liturgical days and seasons, keep the movie in mind, letting its scenes and characters stay with you. Watch for connections, and make note of them when they come to you. Also, in making your pastoral rounds, do any of the characters, scenes, issues, and problems of the film connect with what is happening to the people you know? Has anyone else seen the film? Discuss it, and make notes.

• If you decide to refer to the film in a sermon, in most cases it is best to assume that the congregation has not seen the movie. You may want to tell the story, succinctly, so that people have some idea of the whole, and then focus on a scene, presenting it in detail. Or the single scene may be enough (and less likely to spoil the movie for people who intend to see it!). Keep in mind, this is not discussion or analysis, but more like a replay. Once this image is seen by the congregation, you can work from it. Sometimes the sermon does not work because the preacher has the scene in mind but has not fixed it in the imagination of the congregation before making something of it. First, internalize it yourself and then help the congregation to picture it, to experience the image. Then you can do with it as you will.

This emphasis on the visual and love of the concrete are the points of strong affinity between sermon and cinema. To summarize, and to underscore the difference between putting ourselves in the power of the incarnate Word and merely manipulating experience—a failing to which both preacher and moviemaker are susceptible—I will quote Nathan Scott once more:

> In such a technological culture as our own, where the world is so constantly approached with an intention to manipulate and convert to use, the great besetting affliction, as Heidegger says, is "forgetfulness" of Being. But he considers it to be the special vocation of the poet to lure us out of that forgetfulness by persuading us once again to "pay heed" to the things of this world and simply to revel in their particularity, in their *presence*, in the marvelous inner cohesion whereby they manage to be what they are, rather than something else. When the poet does succeed in thus throttling the manipulative passions and eliciting from us an act of strict attention before What-is, he performs, as Heidegger sees it, a very great service indeed, for in this way he teaches us how to "hail" Being—which is to say that he takes us into the dimension of the Holy.[33]

It is this paying attention to the world, this embodiment of the actual, that is the potential of both picture show and pulpit.

THE THEATER AND PREACHING

The show is not the show, but they who go.
—William Shakespeare

Someone once asked Samuel Miller, then dean of Harvard Divinity School, where he would go to church in New York City to be moved. Miller confessed that he was at a loss to guarantee such a pulpit, but that he could recommend three or four plays. One could use such a story to suggest what is not true: that the pulpit is generally lifeless and in need of stimulation and material from such exciting quarters as Broadway. To take a more positive view, we have only to keep in mind that this high view of theater came from a theologian and preacher. When we consider what preaching is, at its best, and consider what drama is, essentially, then we see that they occupy common ground.[34]

It is beyond the scope of this book to treat historically, theologically, and aesthetically the many congruences between the church's liturgical life and the dramatic arts. The subjects come readily to mind: Drama as we know it was born among the preaching friars of the Middle Ages; Christianity, by virtue of its sacramental and language-oriented theology, is particularly hospitable to the theater as a place where ordinary human experience is both imitated and transcended; the liturgy and the staged play have much in common, in their use of time and space as well as in their combination of the tragic and the comic; the Bible's preachers and storytellers, like the best of our playwrights, are given to imagination but not to sentiment (a prime example would be the parables of Jesus), to passion but not so much to parading feelings or piety; the best sermons, like the best plays—that is, those that have the greatest effect—do not preach. In homiletical and theological reflection on "the Word of God" we speak of the "Word-event," a moment closely analogous to the event for which the playwright strives, when, by imagination, each member of the audience comes and stands on the stage, as part of the action or as one of the characters.

One could, following Tillich, develop these ideas in the context of a theology of culture: Because religion is the substance of culture and culture the form of religion, then obviously such a phenomenon as the theater is of the greatest theological significance.[35] But our interest here is in the more practical matter of taking the preacher to the theater and bringing the play to the pulpit. What follows is a chronicle of an evening at the theater in New York, of moving from that experience toward a sermon, and of the preparation of the sermon. The chronicle also includes a reconsideration of the whole experience. Practical matters and theoretical and theological considerations will appear along the way.

The Play Is the Thing

The Circle Repertory is just off Sheridan Square, and we were no sooner inside on a muggy August evening than we wondered whether for twenty-five dollars we could not have found a more comfortable and cheerful spot somewhere Uptown. But among the off-Broadway shows, *Balm in Gilead* had had the best reviews. We entered past a dirty urinal and public-toilet graffiti only to find ourselves in a down-at-the heels West Side coffee shop that had not been swept, it appeared, any more recently than the streets outside.

Our seats were front-row center, which meant that we were in the middle of the action and soon to be approached by the monte men, smooth talking and flipping their three cards faster than the eye could follow. People around us lost a few dollars: It *was* just like being on the street, especially as the cast of twenty-nine began to take over the coffee shop: prostitutes, pimps, transvestites, junkies and dealers, the new girl on the block, the mentally ill, and the just plain ne'er-do-wells. On the wall was the usual menu, from burgers to breakfast, and such signs as "No Dancing" and "$1 Minimum in Booths." To the right was the washroom through which we had entered; the street people were constantly trying to sneak into it, past the vigilant owner and large counterman. To the left, in shadows and one story above stage, a by-the-hour hotel room.

Though the play lasted more than two hours—and seemed longer—the story is quickly told, what story there is. We actually do not learn much about these people at all, certainly not about their past: They are the people that we pass on the streets of any big city. There is one extended monologue in which Darlene tells us about her life with Cotton, in Chicago, and we get some insight into what has brought her here. But for the most part all we see are broken, lost people coping as best they can on scraps of food and human interaction. The small plot revolves around Joe, whose ambition gets him involved with drugs and the mob, and leads eventually to his death, in the booth where he and Darlene have become regulars. The hit-man, in slacks and sweater, stabs Joe with a foot-long hypodermic needle, three times.

The play is relentless, almost without relief. One woman, nearly comatose from heroine, spends almost the entire play at the counter —the only exception being one trip to the roof for a fix—half on, half off her stool, her grip on the counter as tenacious and precarious as the life that screams and scratches around her. We see, as the play goes on, that she is everyone here, barely able to hang on, waiting for the next fix of one kind or another. Joe and Darlene could be Adam and Eve, or a pair of young lovers anywhere, when they take off their clothes and she rubs his back in the cool hotel room upstairs. And there is now and then a moment when someone seems to listen, or someone laughs. But for the most part, we are left with this scene, nothing closer to balm than a cup of coffee, memories, a needle in the arm.

This staging and the narrow plot achieved what is most important for a play: The audience comes on stage. Entering the theater with the sole intention of extracting material for a sermon can thwart this kind of absorption into the play no less than a preoccupation with being entertained might prevent another the-atergoer from entering into such a play as *Balm in Gilead*. If we move too soon toward finding a sermon we are not likely to en-ter fully into the dramatic action: The difference between vital metaphor—demanding participation—and an illustration that we might superficially manipulate becomes clear here. Walter Wink's advice on parables could as well be said of going to the theater: "To hear a parable . . . means to submit oneself to entering its world, to make oneself vulnerable, to know that we do not know at the outset what it means."[36] The play is the thing. We are called by the play to pay attention and to enter it. Nathan Scott believes that this is the essential goal of all the dramatic arts: "The aim is to see 'the very thing and nothing else'; the principal search (in painting, music, lit-erature, and the cinema) is for what Goethe called the *Urphanomen*; and, in this way, it is hoped that by impaling the imagination on the very things of earth themselves, by 'saving the appearances,' we may save ourselves."[37]

It is this "impaling the imagination on the very things of earth" that holds such great promise for preaching, and calls us to regard the arts as both material and model for the pulpit. So, the play is the thing.

From Stage to Pulpit

On the other hand, we do have this vocation to preach, to witness to a particular tradition in a community of faith. It may be good ad-vice to "simply live, and then go to the pulpit and make something of it." If, however, the play is moving it is likely that the preacher will make a start toward a sermon even during the performance. Or, in the case of a play like *Balm in Gilead*, the preacher may, at first, draw a complete blank. I came away from the play slightly depressed, ill-prepared to face the noise and grime of Manhattan in summer, and far from inspired for the task of preaching. As al-most inevitably happens when one of my theological colleagues is around, someone asked, "Well, did you find a sermon in that?" It was a question best answered by silence.

But, as often happens, the play had its own way, and with time its characters and scenes re-presented themselves as powerful images of struggling, somehow surviving people. More recently, the play has seemed prophetic, an early voice crying out in the wilderness of drugs and violence that now invades our cities. In this regard the stage is like the pulpit: The best sermons are not easily summed up over Sunday dinner, reduced to so many points, so many easily assimilated ideas. It is the event itself—multifaceted, appealing to the imagination, calling for deep participation—that has power. The marks of a great play, as of a compelling sermon, were all there: our emotional and physical participation in day-to-day life; the hard but real humanity, these undeniable people; the unresolved situation crying out for some invading word, some transcendent presence, for more than could be said or done then and there. The play, resisting immediate closure or superficial use, became a potentially redeeming metaphor.

We could probably follow a rule of thumb: The more difficult the play to assimilate, the more promising for preaching, both as model and material. Experience with this play would confirm that. The title itself added to the difficulty. Most churchgoers would expect something overtly religious in a play with that title, and I found myself expecting, half hoping, to hear someone like Mahalia Jackson belting out the familiar spiritual. But the author, Lanford Wilson, held back, kept our noses in the worst of it, gave us the barest hints that he even knew the biblical associations of the title. It was only as days passed that I began to hear some of the lines as the scenes came back. For example, Tyg, in an obscure conversation in the corner, is telling someone that "they had a salve back there in Egypt that could cure most anything." And in time the death of Joe, stabbed three times with a spike-like needle, began also to connect with Scripture.

So the play stayed with me and led eventually to my looking again at the familiar text in Jeremiah. With the play as a foil against which to study the pericope, exegesis took on new life, and certain motifs sprang to attention. For example, in Jer. 8:18—9:1, the prophet gives no suggestion that the calamity of the people is a punishment for sin; rather, he reveals his complete sympathy with the stricken people. Not only is the harvest past, but the season of summer fruits fails also. The metaphor is one of desperation—a desperation not unlike the utter hopelessness to which contemporary sociologists and social psychologists trace much of the escapism and violence in our cities. Surely, says the prophet, there must be relief somewhere, some medicine, some good physician who can help. Maybe from Gilead, the rough hill country east of the Jordan, a place fabled for its healing ointment, could come some balm. Even Jeremiah's motif of summer connected with that hot night in New York, and the prophet's love of dramatic action made me think that he would have applauded Wilson's skill in putting us in the middle of the situation.

In this case, the play led the preacher back to Scripture, and the result was a second look at a well-worn text. This may often be the case with the arts as we are looking for responsible ways to do what Robert Raines calls "raiding the Bible" and "preaching from the inside out."[38] This possibility calls for even better knowledge of Scripture, a dwelling in the Bible that allows us to bring its stories, images, and characters into connection with a secular play. Imaginative preaching demands even greater faithfulness in exegesis and disciplined theological reflection.

Though our preaching will normatively follow the lectionary, we may in fact not always find our sermon starting from Scripture. Once we connect with Scripture, however, what is crucial is that we listen carefully, honestly, contemplating the text in the new light that experience—in this case, of the theater—is bringing to it. It may well be, too, that coming to Scripture by way of a play makes for this deeper, more intense listening. In the precise meaning of the word, *exegesis* refers to a *leading out* of the text. Immersion in a new experience, the theater, might well be one more means of accomplishing this, as "deep calls to deep" and the human realities of our time address their questions to the biblical tradition. Is Robert Raines right in saying that "the Bible is just so much wind until we put up our lives as a sail"? In the case of *Balm in Gilead*, vivid human experience provoked and enabled new attentiveness to the text. This renders somewhat artificial the notion that every sermon must begin with the studious exegesis of a predetermined pericope.

The "rubrics," outlined above, for bringing movies to the pulpit fit the theater as well, as practical suggestions for first letting go, getting on stage and letting the comedy and tragedy of theater take us over, and then bringing that experience to preaching. I have sketched out a good many sermon ideas on a playbill, which I keep as reference for the names of characters and other data.

Often the play remains unfinished. We have experienced, with the players, a circumscribed space and time, "danced a round upon this green," and then the curtain comes down. The play occurs, and that is more important than its being definitive or conclusive. Like any good symbol, the play rises from life and it merges, again, with the ongoing stream of human experience. This is part of its power, that in being sufficiently ambiguous while authentically and recognizably human, the play connects with our lives, creates new experience, and then the curtain comes down.

Dramatic art is closely analogous to liturgy and instructive for the preacher. The concluding chapter addresses several questions related to the qualities that preaching shares the with arts: eventfulness, concreteness, preoccupation with the human, and a driving desire to connect with a congregation or audience. More than literature, cinema, or drama, however, preaching lives in a symbiotic relationship with a particular group of people. In that situation, the highest and most courageous art is required. How can the preacher be as much the voice of a community's liturgical life as the unique human voice is the signature of a man's or woman's bodily life? That is where we conclude, in describing the art of preaching as availability to liturgy.

6
An Available Voice

A poet's hope: to be
like some valley cheese,
local, but prized elsewhere.
—W. H. Auden, "Shorts I,"
Epistle to a Godson

But we have this treasure in earthen vessels....
—2 Cor. 4:7a

Dry wafer,
sour wine.

This day I see
God's in the dust,
not sifted
out from confusion.

Dry wafer,
sour wine:
this day I see
the world, a word
intricately incarnate, offers—
ravelled, honeycombed, veined, stained—
what hunger craves,
a sorrel grass,
a crust,
water,
salt.
—Denise Levertov, "This Day"

The Greek Orthodox cathedral in the old Plaka section of Athens
was dark as the service began before dawn on Sunday morning.

But near my pew, toward the rear of the church, two candles illumined a glowing icon, a larger-than-life face of Christ. Each person who entered the church approached this icon and, before taking a seat, kissed the glass that covered it. An American abroad, my first thought was for sanitation. Soon, however, a woman in black appeared with paper towels and Windex. Every few minutes, during the several hours that people continued to fill the church, she worked at spraying and wiping away the accumulating devotion, seeking clarity in the face of mystery. Here is one more picture of the liturgical situation of preaching.

PREACHING AS LITURGY

The vocation of preaching is not so far from that sexton's lowly office: The preacher attempts language that can only partially unveil but is indispensable to the mystery of faith. Gail Ramshaw-Schmidt describes liturgy as layering, the accumulation of one layer of interpretation upon another: "Some layers illumine and some dull the mystery of Christ."[1] In Ramshaw-Schmidt's way of seeing it, the homily—like various other forms of speech that we use in worship—is "trying out" once more the accumulated language of liturgy:

> The liturgical homily at its best is neither a commercial that breaks up the show, nor the show surrounded by commercials. It is mystagogy, catechesis for the faithful, instruction in how this sacred speech and these holy symbols can be incorporated into contemporary life. The homily allows the preacher—presumably uniquely adept or trained in this skill—to rehearse the sacred images, to try them out, to apply them, this Sunday, to yesterday's crisis or tomorrow's pain.[2]

Preaching is no less liturgical language than prayer or hymnody; the preacher, too, depends for the sacred words and images on the layers of faithful interpretation, tradition. At the same time, however, the preacher is called to a special liturgical vocation and to a holy, if earthy, art.

The Voice of Christ's Body

Whatever shape it takes and whenever it occurs, Christian liturgy is always a communal act, and it always intends to meet Christ, who has promised to be present with those who gather in his name. This is where preaching occurs, as the unique voice of the body of Christ, the church. If we can make this ecclesiological and christological affirmation, then our homiletics will shift more toward a liturgical function.

Every sermon, Joseph Sittler says, is triply organic to its setting: to a time, a place, and to particular personalities. "Preaching is an act of the church in which the substance of her faith is ever freshly declared and reinterpreted to the lives of men who live within the instant and changing actuality of history."[3] Among other things, that means that the sermon is probably a throwaway. If it is art, it is in the genre of the movable, the plastic, and even the ad hoc. The art that has found the largest place in Christian worship is probably music, which has a specific duration, like speech. The sermon happens—neo-orthodoxy was fond of speaking of the "Word-event"—and its temporality is an essential characteristic of its liturgical function, to occur at a specific moment in the ongoing life of a community, in organic connection with flesh and blood people who live in a particular place. The stronger the community's liturgical sense and belief that in the public event of the Eucharist Christ will meet with the church until the end of time, the stronger will be the sense of organic connection between the newly spoken word—the homily for the day—and the community's life. This voice, the preacher, speaks among and for a community that has been saying these words and living with these symbols for a long time, but freshly, so as once more to "try them out" in the face of what is happening to these very people here and now. Preaching, as liturgy, is available to piety, but not captive to it.

A Human Voice

We cannot make too much of the fact that the appearance of the Word in the community is organic to the life a particular person and resonates in a recognizably human voice. The person who can speak—produce sound waves in the larynx that bombard, with no intervening medium, the eardrums of those who listen—possesses the essential instrument of liturgy, an instrument more subtle and versatile than any in the orchestra. In the human voice lie possibilities for recalling the past, meeting the present, and suggesting the future. It is unmatched by palate or pen. In the preacher the Word of God is embodied in a person and concentrated in speech. Preaching, Sittler says, is "a function of the preacher's whole existence concentrated at the point of declaration and interpretation."

This "concentration" at the point of declaration (bringing back the old language, the images, the venerated icon) and interpretation (renewing the tradition and bringing meaning into the clear for us at our time and place) depends upon a person fully alive whose voice comes from the depths of her or his being. One homiletics teacher urges: Come to the pulpit with your heart full and your hands empty. Another tells us to preach from the soles of our feet. Sittler speaks of preaching as "organic to the entire actuality of the preacher," who is one formed by and deeply bonded to Christ's body.[4] This is what we witness when a man or woman stands up to speak the familiar language of Scripture and church, in connection with what we read in the paper this morning or what happened on Main Street Thursday, and suddenly we see more clearly. The voice of Christ's body is always a recognizable human voice available to our life here and now.

PREACHING AS ART

The art of preaching is very largely a function of availability. The preacher's particular gift, stemming from formation in the community and a holy eros for its language and symbols, is the willingness and ability to be keenly open and alive to the community's situation. We could use such words as *awareness, sensitivity,* or even *creativity.* But the notion of being available seems to comprise all of these, and to go further in adding to them a clear intentionality, to be there for these people at the crucial moments, no less in the pulpit than in crisis or celebration.

Improvisation

The French organists specialize in this. I once heard Jean Langlais take a short musical theme, given to him from the audience, and improvise on it for ten or fifteen minutes. The theme is alternately hidden and revealed, obscured by an overlay of what we could call, in Auden's terms, "unlikeness," only to be brought out into the open again with new clarity. This requires, of course, profound musical knowledge, endless preparation, and amazing dexterity. There is about it, too, great playfulness, even at times abandon, and a sharp ear, the keenest listening. Langlais is blind, and I could not help thinking that even his blindness was part of his ability to create on the spot.

The human voice has this remarkable capacity to improvise, and that ability makes the preacher uniquely available to the worshiping community. The sermon does not exist until it is spoken, and the fact that it is spoken allows for improvisation on the spot. The preacher's themes come from the church year, the lectionary, the particular liturgical occasion. The variables in the community's life—the world of the evening news and all the changes to which flesh is subject—call for improvisation. Unless the preacher is available for this, preaching will not fulfill its unique liturgical role.

A Homiletical Failure

The sermon failed—at least was not what it could have been—because it did not improvise on the theme given by the occasion. I traveled to a handsome town in central Pennsylvania, to preach in the university chapel on Sunday morning. It was late October, and the lectionary said it was the twenty-fourth Sunday after Pentecost, but the weather announced on every hand that it was Indian summer. As I strolled to the chapel, vestments over my arm, the dazzling day was already luring undergraduates out into the sunshine.

There was much in the service to match the weather. The chapel itself was sunny and well appointed, with a fine, bright organ and an excellent choir of fresh young voices. A student—even her name was Gold—played the flute and the choir sang a tranquil anthem, "What I profess with my lips, / let me believe in my heart and live in my life." Even the bell choir was at its best. The whole occasion seemed to rejoice in peace and beauty.

I had, of course, prepared well in advance and had come with a finely tuned sermon on the lection, Jesus' parable of the Pharisee and the publican. I teach a course on preaching the parables, and so I was up on my subject. To my preparation had been added a conversation at supper on Saturday night in which a professor told me of contention on campus, groups pairing off against each other. This only reinforced my exegetical theme, focusing on the words of the Pharisee, "I thank you God that I am not like other people." So the sermon spoke of our common humanity, using as a primary metaphor the common cup of the Eucharist (which, I learned later, is not the practice of that community). The sermon ended by reminding the congregation that God in Christ is present to us in each other, that our common humanity is the aim of the gospel, and that God is praised and prayer is authentic when we accept each other rather than exclude, as in the parable.

That sermon fell short of what it might have been. Driving back to New Jersey, I came to see that I had not been sufficiently available to the moment, not ready enough for improvisation on the actual liturgical occasion—which that morning could not help including the weather. Driving along with the benefit of hindsight, I composed a series of rubrics and under each a bit of the sermon that should have been given, and which would have been easy to deliver had I been sufficiently open, aware, and free for improvisation. Here, roughly, is what I composed.

Begin with personal and common experience, with what we are actually experiencing together. "As I walked up to the chapel this morning.... On such a day it is easy to feel that we belong to each other, to the earth, to all that is. Everything around us seems to be saying Yes. Maybe the best we could do would be to put on our shorts and go outside to let the sun bless us."

Deepen the experience—perhaps to a question or a problem—by connecting it to the text. "But we easily forget that the same sun shines on all, that we occupy a common earth. Jesus even told a story of two men at prayer, standing before the one in whom we all live, one praying: 'I thank you that I am not like him. . . .' That no doubt happens, even on this beautiful and well provided campus, in one way or another." [Here I could easily have told a story that I carry around in memory:]

During a recent transit strike, a young man was walking home from work through the park. It was late and he was alone. In the middle of his trek he saw someone approaching him on the path. There was, of course, a spasm of fear: He veered, the stranger veered.

But since they both veered in the same direction they bumped in passing. A few moments later the young man realized that this could hardly have been an accident, and felt for his wallet. It was gone. Anger triumphed and he turned, caught up with the pickpocket, and demanded his wallet. The man surrendered it. When he got home, the first thing he saw was his wallet lying on the bed. There was no way of avoiding the truth: He had mugged somebody.[5]

Affirm the gospel by connecting experience, text, and the tradition. "Jesus, in this parable and by his life, death, and resurrection, gives us the freedom to be together, like people in shorts out on the grass just letting the sun shine on them. Like Mikhail Gorbachev calling his people to *glasnost*, Jesus calls us away from 'old thinking,' and into the glorious liberty of the children of God. We belong to Christ, who has by his death on the cross drawn the whole world to himself, so that in him every human being belongs to us too. If we profess this faith, let us, in the words of the anthem, pray that we may have grace to believe it in our hearts and to live it, even on this campus, in our lives."

The availability of the preacher to the occasion, the willingness and ability to embody the Word for this very time and place, makes all the difference. What was needed that morning, as on most liturgical occasions, was not the set piece but a lively improvisation. As Dag Hammarskjold prayed: "Lord—thine the day, / And I the day's."[6]

Modulation

For a musician modulation is probably less demanding than improvisation. The church organist, for example, may modulate between a hymn and another part of the liturgy, as a kind of musical transition. In speaking, modulation involves a change in tone, and it is, once again, often a matter of sensitivity. It is essential to liturgy, and it is a homiletical art to be cultivated.

An example from the liturgy is the collect that the celebrant may say at the end of the prayers of the people. At this point in the eucharistic liturgy the one presiding may simply use one formula prayer, may select a collect from elsewhere in the service book, or may compose a collect on the spot. The decision made here is an opportunity for liturgical modulation, and it comes in response to the sermon and to the prayers of the people. For example, imagine that at a service in the season after Epiphany, the preacher has focused on a line from the psalm for the day, "The Lord is my light and my salvation, whom shall I fear?" in such a way as to call us to confidence and trust. The collect at the prayers might be the one that begins, "O God, as you have taught us that in quietness and confidence shall be our strength...." That is liturgical modulation. It can occur also in the offertory sentence that calls the people to the Eucharist, and at a number of other points in the liturgy.

But the liturgical function of the sermon itself demands the art of modulation, sensitivity to what is surfacing in this community's life on this very day and even as the service proceeds. Modulation serves the vitality of liturgy, not as innovation but as response to the community's will to pray in the context of its particular situation. As Denise Levertov's poem (see the beginning of this chapter) suggests, each time we come to the Eucharist, we bring the world with us, and the Word adequate to that is "intricately incarnate."

The following is an example of the necessity for homiletical modulation. I had a good sermon all worked out for the chapel of an Episcopal seminary, on the story of Lazarus and the rich man, the Gospel for the day. I had just been to an affair at which we did in fact dress ourselves in finery and "dine sumptuously." But I had also become aware of the will of these suburbanites to find Lazarus, to see him and somehow to connect with him: a young woman leaving her comfortable life to go to seminary, a businessman giving lunch hour to a soup kitchen in Morristown, and the pastor, whose retirement we were celebrating, leaving that affluent parish with a new sense of mission to its neighbors in Newark. I had been reading Robert Bellah, and could not help commenting on his notion of "Sheilaism"—the absolute preoccupation with oneself that prevents our seeing people around us. It was an appropriate sermon for an academic setting, and the congregation could identify with my cast of characters.

The news of the day, however, was the death of John Walker, bishop of Washington, a black man who had been working at two projects, the completion of the National Cathedral and meeting the crisis of poverty, drugs, and crime in the nation's capital. I heard this news in the vestry, just before going in for the service. The very least that was called for that evening was modulation, to let the tone of the sermon somehow find the pitch of that community. Anyone who preaches will have had a similar experience—a death, a crisis, some surprise—but the need for modulation is always there, and we are called to practice this sensitive art as we preach.

At that particular service, had I been more present and lighter on my homilctical feet, I would probably have set most of my sermon aside—relying on the exegetical part to keep the text in view—and followed the community's "story," the compelling event of that moment. To use Ramshaw-Schmidt's language, I could have "tried out" the familiar story of Lazarus and Dives on what had just happened to this community. The best sermon for that occasion would probably have juxtaposed Bishop Walker's struggle to build a cathedral while ministering to the city of Washington, which literally lies at the feet of that great church, with the story of Lazarus lying at the door of the rich man. That kind of modulation demands of the preacher complete availability to the community and its liturgy.

PREACHING AS A LITURGICAL ART

Preaching is related to liturgy in much the same way that cooking is related to a meal with family and friends. Without cooking there could hardly be a meal, but gathering around the table to enjoy the food is the important thing. The best cooks I know have a sense of the whole occasion, so that the planning and preparation of the food are done with the care and energy that come from imagining a lively and beautiful event to which one can contribute a particular skill. Also, a truly accomplished cook understands improvisation: The very best cook I know does not follow recipes. She is constantly reading cookbooks and magazines on food, but when it comes time to go to market and into the kitchen, her work is all freedom and inventiveness.

A Return to Liturgical Speech

When we say homiletics we say liturgics. Preaching is for an occasion, normally for the Sunday-by-Sunday celebration of the resurrection. In some ways this occasion does not vary at all, but at the same time it is constantly moving and changing. The preacher finds a place to stand in its constancy, and is called to the most imaginative and creative work by its movement. This means that liturgy sets limits to preaching, gives it the primary language and essential symbols, at the same time that it calls for improvisation and sensitive modulation. When it comes to actually doing this work, the liturgical art of preaching always entails two essential, sometimes conflicting qualities: preparation and presence.[7]

Preparation. No performance can succeed without preparation, on the stage, in the concert hall, or in the pulpit. The question is not whether preaching is a performance—it obviously is—but how the preacher can perform in a way that forwards the liturgical work of the people. Preparation for the dozen or more minutes that the preacher stands up to speak on Sunday morning is exacting: exegesis, theological reflection, prayer, attentiveness to social and personal experience, designing and writing sermons, disciplined diet, rest, and exercise. Sunday morning will reveal in one way or another the level of preparation, just as one's voice betrays her or his physical condition.

The embodied Word calls for the preparation of one's whole being, including the body, for this holy vocation. Charles Spurgeon, the English preacher, once said that sometimes the Holy Spirit is indistinguishable from a walk in the fresh air: Following his lead I have taken to running on Sunday morning and urging physical fitness on my students as preparation for preaching. Whatever form it takes, without careful, intentional discipline no artist succeeds, and it is as true of the preacher as of the actor or dancer that we must put our whole being, including our bodies, into the task. Preaching, like the common action of the community in the liturgy, is an act that people do with their bodies.[8] Preparation of the sermon is essential, and preparation of the preacher no less so. Preparing the preacher, spiritually and physically, is necessary to the proper balance in preaching between preparation and presence. This second factor, equally important, often is at odds with preparation. I have given examples above of the well-prepared sermon that was somehow unable to enter into a specific liturgical occasion, to take its pulse and respond accordingly, in the moment.

Presence.   Preaching as a liturgical art demands presence, being attuned to the moment. The most carefully prepared sermon, especially the literary set piece, can easily miss the mark if the preacher is not present to the situation at hand. Often the inability to be present comes from insecurity, accumulated stress, the fear of losing one's place, forgetting the sermon, making a faux pas. This insecurity may take the form of staying too close to a manuscript, relying upon the pat illustration in a way that causes one to miss the community's story that is being told right then and there, or undue preoccupation with style. This does not mean that a manuscript cannot serve preaching well or that style is unimportant, but it is at these points that the tension between preparation and presence becomes most often apparent.

In virtually any liturgy, however prescribed the order and set the rite, the sermon is potentially a moment of freedom. The preacher stands up and speaks to people directly, in the moment. Behind this speech lies a venerable tradition, and before it lies the movement of the community toward the holy table. But in its essence it is a person speaking, present here and now, sentient and aware of these particular people in the flesh. It is this personal presence and its medium of speech that give preaching its power within the liturgy. But everything depends, here, upon the preacher—however well prepared—being there in mind, spirit, and body. I believe my sermon fell flat that Sunday morning at a Pennsylvania college because I was not sufficiently there as a *body*, responding in the flesh to the glory of a new morning in a way that would allow the Gospel to shine through our common delight in creation. Preparation—and perhaps some anxiety in being in an academic, nonparochial setting—had, in fact, blocked presence. But when these are in balance, preparation enables presence, and presence takes full advantage of all that has gone into getting the preacher ready to stand up in the pulpit. Aidan Kavanagh could be speaking for the preacher no less than for the presider at worship: "To be consumed with worry over making a liturgical mistake is the greatest mistake of all. . . . One who is careful, informed, and sincere will not have to worry about the liturgy very much."[9] In preaching and liturgy, that is what we aim for, informed and careful preparation that sets us free to make the preacher's particular offering to the work of the people.

RETURN TO THE TABLE

This embodiment, in the moment, of the Word is most accessible in the sacramental community. The presence of the preacher to the community depends upon her or his taking a place with the congregation in the primary work of the community, the regular celebration of the resurrection, the presence of Christ with God's faithful people. Here we can make some progress toward diminishing the place of ego in the pulpit in favor of preaching as the voice of Christ's body, as the voice of a baptized people who are constantly being forgiven and renewed. Here we have the freedom to be available, to the gospel and the community, the freedom of ourselves being formed and nourished in Baptism and Eucharist, the freedom of living in grace. As Luther said, we are never justified by grace more than when we preach!

This means that returning to the table sets the preacher free to be an available voice. Harry Emerson Fosdick described preaching as an animated conversation about real-life situations,[10] a homiletic toward which we are still striving. That way of preaching, open and available, alive to a congregation even in the moment of preaching, is most likely to be achieved by a renewal of the early church's placement of preaching at the table, in the midst of the eucharistic community. Here preaching finds its boundaries, its aim, and its freedom.

Returning to the table, far from turning us toward being an esoteric and exclusive coterie, opens the community and its preacher toward the world. This is being demonstrated across the world where sacramental communities, often house churches, are centers of energy for justice. The Word embodied in the sacramental community seeks further embodiment in the day-to-day world, and living close to the sacraments will have the effect of turning the preacher's eyes more and more toward the world at whose hands Jesus is crucified and whose redemption, through Jesus' death and resurrection, empowers every Eucharist. The sacraments are not just the celebrations of an in-group, rejoicing in their redemption; every Eucharist recalls Jesus nailed to the cross, his arms extended to the whole world, and announces the coming to all people of his gracious reign. Entering every Lord's day into Jesus' death drives the church outward to seek justice, even as the celebration of his resurrection sustains the community in faithful obedience. Holding justice and jubilation together is a sacramental way of being in the world, and this is the shape of Christian preaching no less than of the Eucharist.

This, too, is the place of the preacher's creativity. We should be little interested in making clever sermons or creating literary pieces. As Kavanagh puts it, "The liturgical minister is not the poet but only the reciter of the poet's poem."[11] The eucharistic community calls the preacher to receive the tradition faithfully, to be formed and sustained by it, and then to go, in word and deed, where contemporary people are, where, to use Sittler's words, "man's mind follows the fortunes of his body with absolute seriousness."[12] The preacher's imagination dwells upon the human condition, as it is shown in the newspaper, the electronic media, the neighbors, the arts, but always from the perspective of the preacher having been baptized and sustained in Christ. Auden calls us to seek Christ, the Way, the Truth, and the Life, in what he calls the world of "unlikeness," "anxiety," and "the flesh."[13] This is the world for which Christ died and for which the church meets to pray; it is the world that the sacraments acknowledge in water, bread, and wine; and it is the world in which the preacher's art embodies the saving Word of God.

Pulpit and table need each other. No sermon can encompass the mysteries of faith; every sermon is finally completed at the table. And without the preacher, the table will stand empty not only of bread and wine but also of its deepest meaning. Through earthy and realistic preaching, by bringing the *saeculum* starkly and unabashedly into the holy place, the preacher creates keener hunger for the bread of heaven and the cup of salvation. Might it be that many Christians do not come to the table because preaching does

not create sufficient hunger and thirst, or satisfies superficially?
Do we assume, to our loss, that preaching should meet our needs,
answer our questions, come to satisfying conclusions, rather than
sharpening our hunger, deepening our thirst? Is not the role of
preaching to make us newly aware of our need for the saving presence of Christ, and of our own embodiment of that saving Word
in the world?

> We are the Incarnation,
> all living things,
> word made flesh;
> transcendent thought of God.
> The Holy Spirit by inspiration
> immanent,
> revealed by grace,
> and flesh enfolds the living Deity,
> translating Him and us,
> a glorious Epiphany,
> a suffering, transfigured human face.[14]

Notes

1. PULPIT AND TABLE

1. See Karl Barth, *Church Dogmatics* (Edinburgh: T. and T. Clark, 1936), 1/1:89; for Justin Martyr's account, see Bard Thompson, *Liturgies of the Western Church* (Cleveland: World, 1962), chapter 1.

2. Aidan Kavanagh, *Elements of Rite: A Handbook of Liturgical Style* (New York: Pueblo, 1982), 21.

3. Karl Barth, *Deliverance to the Captives* (New York: Harper, 1961), 19.

4. See Fred B. Craddock, *As One without Authority* (Enid, Okla.: Phillips University, 1971). I will elaborate what I mean by this and provide examples in chapter 6.

5. Quoted by Karl Barth, *Church Dogmatics*, 1/1:107.

6. Ibid., 208.

7. Quoted by Karl Barth, *Church Dogmatics* (Edinburgh: T. and T. Clark, 1956), 1/2:249.

8. Phillips Brooks, *Lectures on Preaching* (New York: E. P. Dutton, 1877), 5.

9. Quoted in Dietrich Ritschl, *A Theology of Proclamation* (Richmond, Va.: John Knox, 1960), 12.

10. Harry Stout, *The New England Soul* (New York: Oxford, 1986).

11. Joseph Sittler, *The Anguish of Preaching* (Philadelphia: Fortress, 1966), 65.

12. Ibid., see chapter 1.

13. Ibid., 65.

14. See Urban T. Holmes, *The Priest in Community* (New York: Seabury, 1978).

15. Sittler, *Anguish of Preaching*, 14.

16. Margaret Craven, *I Heard the Owl Call My Name* (Garden City, N.Y.: Doubleday, 1973); Graham Greene, *The Power and the Glory* (New York: Viking, 1940).

17. H. H. Farmer, *The Servant of the Word* (New York: Scribner's, 1942).

2. THE AMERICAN SITUATION

1. Yngve Brilioth, *A Brief History of Preaching* (Philadelphia: Fortress, 1965), 172.

2. Ibid., 173.

3. See Henry Steele Commager, *The American Mind* (New Haven: Yale University Press, 1950).

4. Phillips Brooks, *Lectures on Preaching* (New York: E. P. Dutton, 1877), 5.

5. Thomas W. Ogletree, *The Use of the Bible in Christian Ethics* (Philadelphia: Fortress, 1983), 3.

6. Harry Emerson Fosdick, *The Modern Use of the Bible* (New York: Macmillan, 1941), 209–10.

7. Ibid., 263.

8. H. Richard Niebuhr, *The Social Sources of Denominationalism* (New York: H. Holt, 1929).

9. Marshall McLuhan, *Understanding Media: The Extensions of Man* (New York: McGraw Hill, 1964), especially chapter 2.

10. Reuel Howe, *Partners in Preaching* (New York: Seabury, 1967).

11. Richard Baxter, *The Reformed Pastor* (Richmond, Va.: John Knox, 1956).

12. See Dietrich Bonhoeffer, *Worldly Preaching*, ed. and trans. Clyde Fant (Nashville: Thomas Nelson, 1975). Bonhoeffer's lectures on homiletics appear on pp. 177ff; there is a new edition of this work (New York: Crossroad, 1991).

13. Brilioth, *Brief History*, 172–74.

3. PREACHING AS A LITURGICAL ACT

1. Interview with Garrison Keillor, *The Wittenburg Door* (December/January 1984–85).

2. Chester Pennington, *God Has a Communication Problem* (New York: Hawthorn, 1976).

3. Vatican II, *Constitution on the Sacred Liturgy*, in Walter M. Abbott, ed., *The Documents of Vatican II* (Piscataway, N.J.: Association, 1966), no. 7.

4. See Bard Thompson, *Liturgies of the Western Church* (Cleveland: World, 1962), chapter 1.

5. Karl Barth, *Church Dogmatics* (Edinburgh: T. and T. Clark, 1936), 1/1:89.

6. Dietrich Ritschl, *A Theology of Proclamation* (Richmond, Va.: John Knox, 1960), 104.

7. Karl Barth, *Church Dogmatics* (Edinburgh: T. and T. Clark, 1956), 1/2:230.

8. Jon Walton, *Word from Westminster: Sermons from Westminster Presbyterian Church* (Wilmington, Del., July 16, 1989), 8.

9. William Skudlarek, *The Word in Worship* (Nashville: Abingdon, 1981), 69.

10. Walter Brueggemann, *The Prophetic Imagination* (Philadelphia: Fortress, 1978), 13.

11. Ibid., 109.

12. Graham Greene, *The Power and the Glory* (New York: Viking, 1940).

13. Edmund Steimle, Morris Niedenthal, and Charles Rice, *Preaching the Story* (Philadelphia: Fortress, 1980), chapter 10.

14. See Geoffrey Wainwright, *Doxology* (New York: Oxford, 1980), chapters 7 and 8.

15. An order for the Great Vigil of Easter can be found in *The Book of Common Prayer* (New York: Church Hymnal Corp., 1979), 285ff.

16. Donald Coggan, *Preaching: The Sacrament of the Word* (New York: Crossroad, 1988), 76–77.

4. A DOWN-TO-EARTH RHETORIC

1. Fred Craddock, *Overhearing the Gospel* (Nashville: Abingdon, 1978), 20.

2. Amos Wilder, *Early Christian Rhetoric* (Cambridge: Harvard University Press, 1971), 68–69.

3. Ibid., 71.

4. John D. Crossan, *In Parables* (New York: Harper and Row, 1973).

5. James Breech, *The Silence of Jesus* (Philadelphia: Fortress, 1983).

6. Wilder, *Early Christian Rhetoric*, 71.

7. See Edmund Steimle, "The Fabric of the Sermon," in Edmund Steimle, Morris Niedenthal, and Charles Rice, *Preaching the Story* (Philadelphia: Fortress, 1980).

8. Paul Ricoeur, "Listening to the Parables of Jesus," in Charles Reagan and David Stewart, eds., *The Philosophy of Paul Ricoeur* (Boston: Beacon, 1978), 239.

9. Wilder, *Early Christian Rhetoric*, 74.

10. Dorothy Sayers, "Towards a Christian Aesthetic," in Nathan Scott, Jr., ed., *The New Orpheus* (New York: Sheed and Ward, 1964), 16–17.

11. Eduard Riegert, "Parabolic Sermons," *The Lutheran Quarterly* 26 (1974), 25.

12. See Joachim Jeremias, *The Parables of Jesus* (New York: Scribner's, 1955).

13. W. B. Yeats, *Ideas of Good and Evil* (New York: Russell and Russell, 1903), 244.

14. Amos Wilder, *Jesus' Parables and the War of Myths* (Philadelphia: Fortress, 1982).

15. H. H. Farmer, *The Servant of the Word* (New York: Scribner's, 1942), especially chapter 3, "Preaching as Personal Encounter."

16. Robert N. Linscott, ed., *Selected Poems and Letters of Emily Dickinson* (Garden City, N.Y.: Doubleday, 1959), 182–83.

17. This discussion was given in part as the William Porcher Dubose lecture at the School of Theology, University of the South, October 11, 1988, published as "Eikon and Eiron: Faith as Imagination," *The Saint Luke's Journal of Theology* 32, no. 4 (September 1989).

18. Morris Niedenthal, "The Irony and Grammar of the Gospel," in Steimle, Niedenthal, Rice, *Preaching the Story*.

19. Nikos Kazantzakis, *The Last Temptation of Christ* (New York: Simon and Schuster, 1960).

20. Crossan, *In Parables*, 13.

21. Ibid., 14.

22. Breech, *Silence of Jesus*, 20.

23. Ibid., 36–37.

24. Craddock, *Overhearing the Gospel*, 99.

25. Breech, *Silence of Jesus*, 99.

26. See Urban T. Holmes, *Ministry and Imagination* (New York: Seabury, 1976).

27. Steimle, Niedenthal, and Rice, *Preaching the Story*, chapter 10.

28. Paul Scott Wilson, *Imagination of the Heart* (Nashville: Abingdon, 1988).

29. Matthew Fox, *Original Blessing* (Sante Fe: Bear, 1983), see especially chapter 23.

30. Breech, *Silence of Jesus*, 53.

31. Gerhard Ebeling, *On Prayer: Nine Sermons* (Philadelphia: Fortress, 1966), 65.

32. See Steimle, Niedenthal, and Rice, *Preaching the Story*, especially the introduction.

5. ART IN THE PULPIT

1. Charles L. Rice, *Interpretation and Imagination: The Preacher and Contemporary Literature* (Philadelphia: Fortress, 1970), xi.

2. Nathan Scott, Jr., ed., *Adversity and Grace* (Chicago: University of Chicago Press, 1968), 15.

3. R. E. C. Browne, *The Ministry of the Word* (Philadelphia: Fortress, 1975), 15.

4. Ibid., 18.

5. See Susanne K. Langer, *Feeling and Form* (New York: Scribner's, 1953).

6. Boris Pasternak, *Doctor Zhivago* (New York: Pantheon, 1958), 10.

7. Interview with John Cheever, *Esquire* 102 (August 1984), 2.

8. Michael Novak, *Ascent of the Mountain, Flight of the Dove* (New York: Harper and Row, 1971), 57.

9. Nathan Scott, Jr., *Modern Literature and the Religious Frontier* (New York: Harper and Brothers, 1958), especially chapter 1.

10. J. D. Salinger, *The Catcher in the Rye* (Boston: Little, Brown, 1951).

11. See Thomas Merton, *Opening the Bible* (Philadelphia: Fortress, 1988).

12. C. S. Lewis, *An Experiment in Criticism* (Cambridge: Cambridge University Press, 1961), 8.

13. Robert Louis Stevenson, *Treasure Island* (New York: Scribner's, 1923).

14. Walter Wink, *The Bible in Human Transformation* (Philadelphia: Fortress, 1973); idem, *Transforming Bible Study* (Nashville: Abingdon, 1980).

15. John D. Crossan, *In Parables* (New York: Harper and Row, 1973), 13.

16. Frederick Buechner, *The Magnificent Defeat* (New York: Seabury, 1968).

17. Frederick Buechner, *The Alphabet of Grace* (New York: Seabury, 1970), 21.

18. Paul Tillich, *Theology of Culture* (New York: Oxford, 1959).

19. Wallace Stevens, "Credences of Summer," quoted in Nathan Scott, Jr., *Negative Capability* (New Haven: Yale University Press, 1969), 221.

20. Crossan, *In Parables*, 11.

21. See Patricia Wilson-Kastner, *Imagery for Preaching* (Minneapolis: Fortress, 1989).

22. Phillips Brooks, *Lectures on Preaching* (New York: E. P. Dutton, 1877), 20ff.

23. Amos Wilder, *Theopoetic* (Philadelphia: Fortress, 1976), 1.

24. For a discussion of a very similar process, see Paul Scott Wilson, *Imagination of the Heart* (Nashville: Abingdon, 1988).

25. Harvey Cox, "Theological Reflections on Cinema," in Nathan Scott, Jr., ed., *The New Orpheus* (New York: Sheed and Ward, 1964), 343.

26. Ibid.

27. Ibid., 355–56.

28. Sallie McFague, *Speaking in Parables* (Philadelphia: Fortress, 1975), 120, 124.

29. Quoted by Amos Wilder, *Early Christian Rhetoric* (Cambridge: Harvard University Press, 1971), 71.

30. Wilder, *Early Christian Rhetoric*, 76–77.

31. Cox, "Theological Reflections," 357.

32. For an example of sermon as critique see Charles L. Rice, "Easy Rider," in Rice, *Interpretation and Imagination*, 145–46.

33. Nathan Scott, Jr., *The Wild Prayer of Longing* (New Haven: Yale University Press, 1971), 74.

34. For further discussion of these themes, see Charles L. Rice, "The Theater and Preaching," *Journal for Preachers* 8, no. 1 (Advent, 1984), 19–25, portions of which are reprinted here.

35. See Rice, *Interpretation and Imagination*, especially chapter 1 and the sermon on Lorraine Hansberry's *A Raisin in the Sun*.

36. Wink, *Transforming Bible Study*, 161.

37. Scott, Jr., *Negative Capability*, 22.

38. Robert Raines, unpublished lecture (Paper delivered at conference on "Training in the Art of Preaching," Kirkridge Retreat and Study Center, Bangor, Pa., June 1988).

6. AN AVAILABLE VOICE

1. Gail Ramshaw-Schmidt, *Christ in Sacred Speech* (Philadelphia: Fortress, 1986), 18.

2. Ibid., 113.

3. Joseph Sittler, *The Anguish of Preaching* (Philadelphia: Fortress, 1966), 7.

4. Ibid., 8.

5. Ibid., 10.

6. Jenna Orkin, "True Tales of New York," *New York*, September 1, 1980, 24.

7. Dag Hammarskjold, *Markings* (New York: Alfred Knopf, 1966), 168.

8. I am indebted for this analysis of performance to Paul Bernabeo, unpublished paper (Delivered at Union Theological Seminary, New York, 1975).

9. See Bernard O. Brown, "Liturgy and the Human Future," *Criterion* 15, no. 3 (Autumn 1976).

10. Aidan Kavanagh, *Elements of Rite: A Handbook of Liturgical Style* (New York: Pueblo, 1982), 31.

11. Harry Emerson Fosdick, *The Living of These Days* (New York: Harper and Row, 1956), chapter 5.

12. Kavanagh, *Elements of Rite*, 94.

13. Sittler, *Anguish of Preaching*, 35.

14. See the second epigraph for chapter 5.

15. Anna Kirby, "Epiphany I," in *The Dust of God* (Lewiston, N.Y.: Edwin Mellen, 1989), 31.